What people are ~~~, ~

QUESTIONING CIRCUMCISION:
A JEWISH PERSPECTIVE

"Thorough, moving, convincing, and of staggering importance. I believe this book will change Judaism for the better." —Michael Koran, Jewish educator

"Jewish circumcision has traditionally been the province of males. This groundbreaking book sheds new light on the issue by also including women's views and feelings about circumcision."
—Rabbi Lynn Gottlieb, Nahalat Shalom Congregation

"For thousands of years we have ceremoniously circumcised our sons without knowing or honestly considering how this practice affects the child. In this book, Ronald Goldman presents us with compelling new information that we can't ignore." —Rabbi Beverly Lerner, psychotherapist

"Goldman's analysis of Jewish reluctance to discuss circumcision is right on the mark. The collective Jewish psyche will benefit from confronting circumcision anxieties and myths. This book will facilitate that process and should lead to more than a few changes of heart and mind."
—Dr. Richard Schwartzman, psychiatrist

"A bold, compassionate, and powerful critique of Jewish circumcision. With revealing new research, Goldman calls attention to the unrecognized physical and psychological effects connected with this procedure."
—Myron Sharaf, Ph.D., lecturer and author, Department of Psychiatry, Harvard Medical School

"The information in this book was the most comprehensive we found. It was very useful in our decision not to circumcise. And after my father read it, he said he could really understand our feelings. I am certain that we made the right decision." —Aviva Furman, mother of uncircumcised son

Voices from *QUESTIONING CIRCUMCISION: A JEWISH PERSPECTIVE*

"If a woman is made to distrust her most basic instinct to protect her newborn child, what feelings can she ever trust?"

—Miriam Pollack,
mother of two circumcised sons

"My son screamed. Unmistakable screams of pain. Sounds I'd never heard from him before. . . . I was in a state of shock."

—Victor Schonfeld,
father of circumcised son

"I experienced my doubts privately and without comfort. . . . Thus, a rite intended to inspire feelings of Jewish unity evoked in me a sense of loss and alienation."

—Lisa Braver Moss,
mother of circumcised son

"I fell in love with my son the first seven days. There was no way we were going to hurt him. . . . We got respect for putting our values into practice."

—Moshe Rothenberg,
father of uncircumcised son

"Every time I change his diaper, I feel so good that we didn't do it."

—Dana Parmes-Katz,
mother of uncircumcised son

"Although uncircumcised, I am a very proud Jew, with a very strong sense of Jewish identity, and never hesitate to affirm my Jewish identity to Jew and non-Jew alike."

—Alan Altmann,
uncircumcised Jew

"When I explained circumcision to him, his face took on a frightened expression as he cupped his hands over his genitals and loudly declared, 'That is never going to happen to me!'"

—Rosemary Romberg,
relating the response of her seven-year-old uncircumcised son

QUESTIONING CIRCUMCISION
A Jewish Perspective

ALSO BY RONALD GOLDMAN

Circumcision: The Hidden Trauma
How an American Cultural Practice
Affects Infants and Ultimately Us All

The Circumcision Resource Center is a nonprofit educational organization with the purpose of providing information and support to the public and professionals concerning the practice of circumcision. The Center offers publications, consultation, telephone counseling, lectures, and seminars. For more information contact

Circumcision Resource Center
P.O. Box 232
Boston, MA 02133
(617) 523-0088

QUESTIONING CIRCUMCISION

A Jewish Perspective

Ronald Goldman, Ph.D.

VANGUARD PUBLICATIONS
Boston

Vanguard Publications
P.O. Box 8055
Boston, MA 02114

01 00 99 98 97   5 4 3 2 1

Line drawings in Figures 2 and 4–8 are used with permission of Edward Wallerstein © 1980

Cataloging-in-Publication Data

Goldman, Ronald.
    Questioning circumcision : a Jewish perspective / Ronald Goldman.
    p. cm.
    Includes bibliographical references and index.
    ISBN 0-9644895-6-2

    1. Circumcision—Religious aspects—United States. 2. Judaism—United States—
Customs and Practices. 3. Berit Milah. I. Title.

BM705.G65 1997   296.4'442   97-40162

Discounts are available on bulk purchases of this book. Excerpts can also be
created to fit your specific needs. Contact the publisher for more information.

Contents

Foreword

Generally, we circumcise our sons without really knowing the effects of what we are doing. We prefer to think of circumcision as a trivial matter. We believe that because it has been done for so many years by so many, that it must be harmless. This book eloquently and effectively questions these assumptions. For the first time, *Questioning Circumcision: A Jewish Perspective* provides the Jewish community with a clear, rational, and sensitive examination of this practice. Dr. Goldman discusses all the aspects of Jewish circumcision that would be of interest to most Jews.

I learned a lot from reading this book. In recent years researchers have discovered much about infants and the effects of surgical procedures on them. (Whether there is a religious ritual or not, circumcision is a surgical procedure.) There is also evidence that infant circumcision can have long-term effects lasting even into adulthood. Dr. Goldman presents this new information in a lucid, well-documented discussion.

Questioning Circumcision: A Jewish Perspective is not just the view of one person. It contains the words of dozens of Jews, including rabbis past and present, who question circumcision. There are many compelling statements made by those who have witnessed circumcisions and have been circumcised. Their words and feelings give us reason to pause and reflect.

The author's psychological approach to the topic is especially valuable. It is exactly what we need to take a close look not only at ritual circumcision, but also at ourselves. With insight, understanding, and compassion, this book answers questions we have been afraid to ask, and asks questions that have not yet occurred to us.

For some readers, the contents of this book will confirm what you have felt for decades. For others, this book will challenge much of what you believe. Whatever your feelings are regarding circumcision, this book can affect you profoundly.

Questioning Circumcision: A Jewish Perspective speaks for many more of us than we are willing to admit. It performs a great service to Jews because it opens a long overdue discussion. I agree with Dr. Goldman that questioning circumcision will ultimately benefit and strengthen the Jewish community.

I highly recommend *Questioning Circumcision: A Jewish Perspective* particularly to expectant mothers and fathers early in their pregnancy so that they may have ample time to ponder its contents. I also recommend it to rabbis who counsel on the merits of circumcision, so they can offer a more informed perspective on this ritual.

Rabbi Raymond Singer, Ph.D.
Neuropsychologist

Introduction

From a global perspective, most of the world does not practice male infant circumcision: about 95 percent of the world's male infants are not circumcised.* Most circumcised men are Muslim or Jewish. The United States is the only country in the world that circumcises most of its male infants for nonreligious reasons.

Routine circumcision of male infants in hospitals in the United States has been increasingly questioned in recent years.[1] In its latest report, the American Academy of Pediatrics found no proven health benefit from circumcision (see Chapter 2).[2] New information, the movement toward natural childbirth, and scrutiny of unnecessary or doubtful surgical procedures have had the effect of reducing the American rate of circumcision over the last two decades from a high of about 85 percent to a current rate of about 60 percent.[3]

Recent medical reports critical of routine male infant circumcision appropriately avoid discussing the religious aspects of circumcision. However, as the American public debate about circumcision develops, Jews are taking a closer look at the practice.

The circumcision debate in the Jewish community is visible and growing. Articles and letters to the editor questioning circumcision have appeared in national Jewish periodicals and newspapers, and an increasing number of Jews are choosing not to circumcise their sons.[4] Some Jewish thinkers have been openly critical of circumcision. Educator and author Howard Eilberg-Schwartz, has written, "Whatever we say that circumcision means, . . . I no longer believe such a wounding is defensible."[5]

---

* Muslims generally circumcise later in childhood.

Yet for those Jews who are expecting a child and who want to explore their options, support for not circumcising their son can still be relatively hard to find.

The purpose of this book is to offer a clear understanding of what circumcision involves, to raise awareness about various concerns, and to encourage Jews to take another look at our assumptions and feelings about circumcision. Though many readers will probably be expecting a child, I would hope that the larger Jewish community would also recognize a need for considering some of the questions raised here. The practice of circumcision really concerns all of us.

It is important to point out a basic difference among Jews. We tend to fall into two main groups, which, for the purposes of this book, shall be called traditionalists and reformists (see Fig. 1). Traditionalists believe that the Torah (the first five books of the Scriptures) is the word of God, and accept it as unimpeachably true. They strictly adhere to Jewish law and observance.

Rabbi Milton Steinberg, in his classic book *Basic Judaism*, writes that, from a reformist (Steinberg uses the word *modernist*) perspective, the Torah

> is a composite of several documents done by diverse authors and sewn into unity by some unknown editor or editors. . . . Some, generally the earliest, are heavily weighted with the folk-lore of the ancient Jews, their rudimentary science and sometimes naive notions of God and morality. Others are consistently on the highest plane.[6]

(The mention of circumcision occurs in one of the earlier documents of the Torah.)

Reformists who are observant generally evaluate an idea not solely based on its conformance with the Torah, but also in light of its agreement with reason and experience. They believe that Jewish practice must be consistent with what they think and feel.

Reform Jews comprise a large proportion of reformists. A descriptive brochure about Reform Judaism affirms that "one of the guiding principles of Reform Judaism is the autonomy of the individual. A Reform Jew has the right to decide whether to subscribe

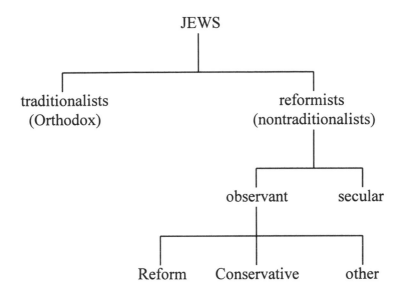

Fig. 1

to this particular belief or to that particular practice. . . . Judaism has never demanded uniformity of belief or practice."[7] Rabbi Eugene Borowitz, noted theologian and scholar, states that Reform Jews "believe that we serve God best by being true to our minds and consciences even where, in significant matters, they clash with our heritage."[8] According to the Union of American Hebrew Congregations, a religious and educational organization that supports Reform Judaism, "Reform Judaism insists that creativity and progress are essential to religious life and that each generation must seek to bring contemporary expression to beliefs and practices of its religious tradition."[9]

A high proportion of American Jews agree with the reformist perspective. According to the Council of Jewish Federations 1990 National Jewish Population Survey, "ninety percent define being Jewish as being a member of a cultural or ethnic group." Less than half associated their Jewish identity with religion. Only 13 percent believe "the Torah is the actual word of God." According to the survey, the general trend is away from traditional Judaism and toward a reformist approach.[10]

Questioning Circumcision: A Jewish Perspective is written from the reformist viewpoint and is intended particularly for reformist Jews. It addresses the main concerns that reformist Jews are examining. Because I include among reformists both observant and secular Jews, certain parts of the discussion may have more appeal to one group than the other.

Many events contributed to my interest in circumcision. I grew up in a predominantly Jewish community and remember first being curious about circumcision when I was about eleven years old. I was reading a book on sex and saw a diagrammatic illustration of an uncircumcised penis. It made no sense to me. I did not know how to reconcile the drawing with how my penis looked. I simply dismissed the illustration and remained puzzled.

About twenty-five years later I was invited to my first bris (ritual circumcision). As one who is very sensitive to the pain experienced by children, I was reluctant to go, but I attended in order not to offend the family. The event is indelibly impressed on my mind. The infant was born naturally without any drugs given to the mother. I learned later in my research into the medical literature that this had an effect on his response to being circumcised. I remember the sound of his cry. I can't imagine an infant crying any louder or with more agony, pain, and sense of urgency in his voice. Using every bit of energy he had, the infant protested vehemently what was being done to him with the best of adult intentions. A few people were crying quietly, including the parents.

Most observers were silent. Discomfort and anxiety permeated the room. I retreated to the kitchen, the farthest I could get from the living room where the cutting was taking place. A young woman who was also in the kitchen sympathized with my feelings of questioning this practice. I wanted to protest to others what was happening, but I restrained myself because I believed that people would not listen to me. This conflict caused me much distress. I resolved never to attend another bris.

I also resolved to do something about what I had witnessed. My subsequent reflection, study, and experience with this issue have convinced me that there are extremely important aspects of circumcision that are not being recognized. My realization motivated me to found the Circumcision Resource Center, a nonprofit educational organization. I have since had hundreds of contacts with men, parents, and mental health and medical professionals. Small group meetings with circumcised men, clinical experience, and independent surveys of attitudes toward circumcision have contributed to a greater understanding of the deep feelings some people have about circumcision.

Circumcision is "normal" among Jews and Americans. Normality is associated with cultural values. What is familiar becomes a cultural value. Circumcision is familiar. The words we use and the words we avoid when talking about a cultural value like circumcision serve to reinforce the practice. Words not typically associated with circumcision may stir uncomfortable feelings, yet a closer look tends to support the connection.

For example, the term "uncircumcised" suggests that to be circumcised is the norm, the standard. This is an assumption made by a culture that practices circumcision. However, as mentioned earlier, nonreligious circumcision is not "normal" in any culture outside of the United States. From a global perspective, to be "uncircumcised" is to be normal, the way males are born, and the way most of the world's males remain.

As the American debate about circumcision develops, the words "intact" and "natural" are being used in place of "uncircumcised" to reflect this global view. This book uses the three words interchangeably. "Intact" means "not altered, complete, whole." "Natural" means "formed by nature, inborn, in its original state." For various reasons we generally do not recognize that the circumcised penis is not natural or intact. As explained in this book, circumcision results in a significant difference.

The arguments in favor of circumcision are familiar and readily available. Previous books on Jewish circumcision have been totally supportive of the practice. It has been rare that writing on Jewish circumcision has mentioned, let alone elaborated on, arguments against the practice. Generally, the Jewish press continues to be very resistant to accepting articles questioning circumcision.

Because the reasons to question circumcision are not well known, they are the focus here. If necessary, I encourage readers to seek other sources of information and then come to their own conclusions. An obvious source would be parents of circumcised sons. In addition, the bibliography includes many sources that support circumcision. For more information on the medical issues, refer to books by Edward Wallerstein and Rosemary Romberg in the bibliography. Their books are out of print but may be available in libraries. A current comprehensive medical review is available from Robert Van Howe, M.D., P.O. Box 1390, Minoqua, WI 54548.

There is much new information in this book. I suggest that you read only as much as you can assimilate without feeling overwhelmed. The emotions that may surface are complex and require time for expression and integration. Consider taking a break from reading when you feel it would be helpful. There is much to think and talk about. Often learning about circumcision raises more and deeper questions. For those who want to explore further, the psychological and social aspects of circumcision are investigated in my book *Circumcision: The Hidden Trauma; How an American Cultural Practice Affects Infants and Ultimately Us All.*

I hope that *Questioning Circumcision: A Jewish Perspective* will stimulate further discussion of this important subject. We owe it to our children to educate ourselves and do what is best for them.

1

Origins and Background

Since many reformist Jews are unfamiliar with the background of the circumcision ritual, a discussion of the origins of circumcision in Judaism will provide the necessary history and also establish a broader context for our discussion of contemporary circumcision issues in subsequent chapters.

The religious origin of the Jewish practice of circumcision is first mentioned in the Torah where God promised Abraham, the first Jew,

> I will make you exceedingly fertile, and make nations of you; and kings shall come forth from you. . . . I assign the land you sojourn in to you and your offspring to come, all the land of Canaan, as an everlasting holding. I will be their God. . . . Such shall be the covenant between Me and you and your offspring to follow which you shall keep: every male among you shall be circumcised. You shall circumcise the flesh of your foreskin, and that shall be the sign of the covenant between Me and you. And throughout the generations, every male among you shall be circumcised at the age of eight days. As for the homeborn slave and the one bought from an outsider who is not of your offspring, they must be circumcised, homeborn and purchased alike. Thus shall My covenant be marked in your flesh as an everlasting pact. (Gen. 17:6–13)

Based on these verses, circumcision is the sign of the covenant between God and the Jewish people, and Abraham was the first circumcised Jew. In its purest sense, Jewish circumcision is an act based on belief in this covenant.

Metaphorical references to circumcision in other biblical verses (e.g., Jeremiah 6:10) suggest a belief that circumcision removes a barrier to proper functioning.[1] (We will examine the effect of circumcision on function in Chapter 4.) In response to the question of why males are not born circumcised, early rabbinic Judaism explains that God created man "incomplete" so that we could finish the work of creation by circumcising.[2]

History

Reformists, of course, consider other perspectives, such as historical, anthropological, and psychological approaches, in examining the origins of circumcision. Jewish historians, for example, acknowledge that Jews did not invent circumcision. The practice was actually well established in ancient Egypt over 6000 years ago.[3] Abraham is believed to have lived around 3600-3800 years ago.[4] However, the oldest written sources of the Torah date from about 3000 years ago, close to three hundred years after the Jews fled from Egypt.[5] The reference in Genesis 17 to "kings shall come forth from you" was probably written a few hundred years later since kings were common in Israel approximately 2500 years ago.[6] Therefore, the Jewish practice precedes the date when it was documented in the Torah by over a thousand years.

Rabbi Lawrence A. Hoffman, professor of liturgy at Hebrew Union College–Jewish Institute of Religion in New York, has studied early Bible texts in detail. He also concludes that circumcision was a custom among Jews long before it became written down and associated with the covenant. Rabbi Sherman Wine agrees that

> by the time the Torah text containing the circumcision command-ment was written, circumcision was so much a part of Jewish prac-tice that no explanation for its choice as the sign of the covenant was required.[7]

Rabbi Hoffman writes that, according to early rabbinic texts, it appears that circumcision was just a physical procedure followed by a meal.[8] Circumcision as a religious ritual started somewhere in the first or second centuries in the *chavurot* (pl.), a new Jewish custom that consisted of groups meeting to share meals and observe life-cycle events.

Around the ninth century the circumcision ritual was performed in the synagogue. The mother traditionally held the infant on her lap during the circumcision. A tendency to exclude the mother from the ritual started around the thirteenth century supposedly because, according to Rabbi Samson of Germany, circumcision was a commandment to be implemented by men, and it was "not appropriate to allow a beautifully dressed-up woman to be among the men and right there in the presence of God."[9]

Anthropological and Psychological Explanations

Several alternative explanations have been offered to account for the origins of Jewish circumcision. The rite could be interpreted as a token sacrifice to God. In ancient times the first-born son was sacrificed to redeem future children in the family (Exod. 22:28).[10] As the culture advanced, this practice was replaced by animal sacrifice (e.g., goat, lamb, bull, sheep, and bird). David Biale, chair of Jewish Studies at the Graduate Theological Union in Berkeley, California, has referred to circumcision as a "substitute sacrifice."[11]

Rabbi Stanley Chyet, a historian and educator, and Rabbi Norman Mirsky, an educator and author who writes about contemporary Jewish life, offer this explanation of sacrifice:

> Human beings must do what they can to win the favor of the divine powers—at the least, to mitigate their enmity—and it is sacrifice, of what is precious to the individual and the collectivity, that has always been seen to achieve this aim. . . . It is through sacrifice that salvation comes; circumcision, in this context at least, is manifestly a salvationary rite, performed by the father on his son to save his—the father's—life, to win him—the father—the divine favor.[12]

Howard Eilberg-Schwartz, in an article with an anthropological perspective, writes that the meaning of the Jewish circumcision ritual is the same as in African circumcision ceremonies: fertility, masculinity, and genealogy.[13] In any case, the significance of circumcision is not inherent in the act. It comes from the meaning that people attach to the practice.

For traditionalists the primary requirement of the circumcision ritual, aside from the cutting of the foreskin, is drawing blood during the procedure. This is reflected in Jewish law that requires that a drop of blood be taken from an infant's penis if he is born without a foreskin. In addition, men who convert to Judaism must have token blood taken from the penis if they are already circumcised. In his 1949 book about circumcision, Joseph Lewis wrote that "circumcision came into existence among the early Hebrews as a blood sacrifice. . . . It was a blood sacrifice on behalf of the boy to cleanse himself of the contamination of having come in contact with the mother's 'uncleanliness.' "[14] According to the Torah, a woman who gives birth to a boy

> shall be unclean seven days; she shall be unclean as at the time of her menstrual infirmity. . . . She shall remain in the state of blood purification for thirty-three days: she shall not touch any consecrated thing, nor enter the sanctuary until her period of purification is completed. (Lev. 12:2, 4)

(A woman who gives birth to a girl shall be "unclean" for twice as many days [Lev. 12:5].)

Eilberg-Schwartz notes that, based on the relevant Torah verses, circumcision "is a rite that marks the passage from the impurity of being born of women to the purity of life in a community of men."[15] This attitude toward women in the Torah reflects the patriarchal traditions of early Judaism.

Barbara Walker, author of several books on women's wisdom and ancient rituals, offers another explanation for circumcision.

> There is much evidence that formal sacrifices of males first arose from a misguided attempt to redesign male bodies to a female model, possibly in the hope of acquiring the female power of reproduction. . . . After the male role in reproduction was finally recognized,

castration of men for religious reasons was gradually abandoned. . . . Circumcision was the usual substitute.[16]

Rabbi Samuel Glasner, past member of the Board of Jewish Education in Baltimore, wrote of circumcision, "We recognize that its origins, even religiously speaking, are primitive and barbaric."[17] The numerous theories about the anthropological origin and purpose of circumcision include associations with sacrifice, fertility, symbolic castration, simulation of menstruation, and male bonding ritual. We cannot identify which one came first. However, because these purposes are consciously seldom used today, we can recognize them as only cultural beliefs. (We do not see our own cultural beliefs so clearly. See Chapter 2.) Typically, they serve to justify an existing practice rather than explain the true origin.

As a psychologist, my own speculative answer to the question of the origin of Jewish circumcision relates to the Torah account, specifically Genesis 17:12–13: "As for the homeborn slave and the one bought from an outsider who is not of your offspring, they must be circumcised, homeborn and purchased alike." This reference to circumcising slaves may have derived from the long-standing custom of mutilating slaves as a way of tangibly marking their subjugation.[18]

I would point out that circumcision is not something people typically volunteer to do to themselves. It is usually forced on them by others who are stronger and in control. The ancient Jews might have "learned" circumcision from the Egyptians when Jews were slaves in Egypt.[19] Upon gaining freedom, circumcised fathers could have chosen to continue circumcising their sons so that their penises would appear similar.* (The covenant was written hundreds of years later.) Today "matching" the father is a major reason given by parents who choose routine American hospital circumcision.[20] Perhaps Jewish circumcision is considered the father's responsibility (rather than the mother's) because of his desire to have his son's penis look similar to his. The father's compliance

---

* I asked a Reform rabbi why he circumcised his son. He told me that religion had nothing to do with it: "I wanted him to look like me."

with the Jewish practice is interpreted as a demonstration of his loyalty to Judaism.

Ascribing a divine commandment to circumcision could have served to relieve the parents of any sense of responsibility or guilt. (Such feelings are reported by parents in Chapter 5.) As a contemporary example, Rabbi Zalman Schachter-Shalomi, a leading voice of Jewish spiritual renewal, expresses his "anguish" over the circumcision decision: "I cannot take the whole responsibility on myself. . . . I need God's command."[21]

Circumcision Has Not Always Been Practiced

Whatever the origin and motivation for Jewish circumcision, contrary to common belief, the rite has not always been practiced. For example, Moses failed to circumcise his son (Exod. 4:25), and circumcision was totally neglected during the forty-year period in the wilderness (Josh. 5:5). In addition, some Jews in the Hellenistic and Roman periods (circa 300 B.C.E.–100 C.E.) chose not to circumcise their sons in an attempt to gain public acceptance.[22]

In 1843 leaders of the Reform movement in Frankfort, Germany, tried to stop circumcision. In addition to arguing that circumcision had not always been practiced, this group of mostly intellectuals and professionals noted that (1) circumcision was not commanded to Moses; (2) the practice is not unique to Jews since Moslems also do it; (3) it is mentioned only once in the Mosaic law and not repeated in Deuteronomy; and (4) there is no comparable practice for females.[23] Some Jewish fathers were also concerned about health risks associated with the procedure. In place of circumcision, Joseph Johlson, a community school teacher, created a ritual called "The Sanctification of the Eighth Day," the first egalitarian Jewish ceremony for male and female infants without genital cutting.[24] Yet when the Reform rabbis met in 1844, the subject of circumcision was considered so controversial that they unanimously agreed not to discuss it.[25]

The controversy over circumcision persisted. Rabbi Abraham Geiger, a leading German reformer of the time, argued that circumcision "fills the father with anxiety and puts the new mother into a state of morbid tension."[26] In a private letter, Rabbi Geiger wrote,

> I must confess that I cannot comprehend the necessity of working up a spirit of enthusiasm for the ceremony merely on the ground that it is held in general esteem. It remains a barbarous bloody act . . . ; the sacrificial idea which invested the act with sanctity in former days has no significance for us. However tenaciously religious sentiment may have clung to it formerly, at present its only supports are habit and fear, to which we certainly do not wish to erect any shrines.[27]

In 1844 Rabbi Samuel Holdheim, another leading reformer, published a pamphlet on circumcision in which he affirmed that circumcision was not a requirement of Judaism.[28] A few years later he wrote that

> protest must be lodged against circumcision, the expression of an outlived idea. . . . I am opposed to circumcision on principle and declare every Jew who confides in my religious insight and conscientiousness, absolved from all obligation in this matter. Yes, I declare every Jew who neglects to have his son circumcised because of his larger belief to be a true and complete Jew.[29]

Parents continued to object to the practice, and the number of uncircumcised children grew.[30] Public opposition to circumcision was expressed in other European countries in the 1840s. Ignac Einhorn, a Hungarian rabbi, proposed that circumcision be replaced with a "spiritual consecration."[31] Olry Terquem, an assimilated French Jew, wrote pamphlets and newspaper articles about "the dangers of circumcision."[32] Furthermore, in 1866 a group of sixty-six Jewish physicians notified the community council in Vienna of their opposition to the practice.[33] A few years later, an Austrian delegate at an assembly of laity and rabbis stated that a common view of parents was, "Our children shall continue to be Jews, but we shall not let them be circumcised."[34] Theodor Herzl, founder of the movement to establish a Jewish state, was one of the most prominent figures who did not circumcise his son, born in 1891.[35]

Currently, circumcision is not universal among Jews outside the United States. A woman who grew up in a traditional Jewish family in France, where many Jews do not circumcise, reported that no male in her large family or among her friends was ever circumcised.[36] Furthermore, some immigrants from South America to Israel are not circumcised.[37]

Changing the Circumcision Procedure

Another widespread misunderstanding about circumcision is that the procedure has always been the same. Originally, only the tip of the foreskin was cut ("You shall circumcise the flesh of your foreskin" [Gen. 17:11].) This practice was called *milah* and lasted about 2000 years. During the Hellenistic period, nudity was popular at public bathing, exercise facilities, and at sports events, and a circumcised penis was considered offensive (see Appendix E). As a result many young Jews altered the appearance of their foreskins by drawing the skin on the shaft forward and tying or pinning it in place.[38] Concealing one's circumcision was quite common. Celsus, author of a first-century medical text, used a surgical procedure called epispasm to disguise circumcision. It involved cutting around the glans (head of the penis) and pulling the shaft skin forward to cover it.[39]

In response to this development, the rabbis of the time decided to specify requirements for the procedure so that a circumcised male could not possibly be altered to appear uncircumcised.[40] This was the start of *periah*, removal of the entire foreskin. Circumcision as it is typically practiced today is based on this historical modification in the procedure.

Interestingly, today in Israel two forms of circumcision are practiced. An Israeli reports that doctors trained in the West remove the entire foreskin, whereas traditional ritual circumcisers remove much less skin.[41]

2

Assumed Benefits

Many circumcision decisions are based on contemporary consid-
erations, which are entirely different from religious beliefs. Rabbi
Joel Roth is a professor of Talmud and rabbinics at the Jewish
Theological Seminary of America and heads the Committee on
Jewish Law and Standards of the Rabbinical Assembly. He ac-
knowledges,

> Once the command [to circumcise] of the covenant is no longer
> determinative, objections to its observance are no longer so easily
> answered. Now the burden of proof is not on those who ignore the
> [circumcision] ritual but on those who observe it. [1]

Justifying circumcision in this case, says Roth, is "an extremely
difficult demand." (He suggests that medical benefits, personal
meaningfulness, and ethnic ties are possible considerations that
may justify circumcision for some parents.)

As the debate over circumcision within Judaism builds, some
Jewish writers are trying to satisfy that demand by defending the
practice on rational and emotional grounds. Cantor Mark Kushner,
for example, makes an emotional appeal when he points out that
in the past some Jews risked their lives and even died to circumcise their sons. [2] One response to this argument is that we can
admire the commitment of those Jews to their beliefs, but they did
not know what we now know about circumcision, and today some
Jews do not share those beliefs.

Jewish Survival and Identity

Another defense for Jewish circumcision is that it ensures the survival of the Jewish people.[3] This contention is especially compelling because of our long history of having to fight to survive as a people. But the biggest threat to Jewish survival today is assimilation. According to the National Jewish Population Survey, more than half of all Jews who married between 1985 and 1990 chose a non-Jewish spouse.[4] Twenty-five years earlier the figure was less than 10%. There is no evidence that circumcision prevents or slows assimilation. (Chapter 6 includes a discussion of Jewish male-female relationships.)

Associated with the desire for survival is the idea of identity. Many Jews believe that males must be circumcised to be Jewish. This is not true. As stated in the *Encyclopedia Judaica*, "It [circumcision] is not a sacrament, and any child born of a Jewish mother is a Jew, whether circumcised or not."[5] The identity argument is further weakened by the fact that in the United States, as well as in Muslim countries and elsewhere, non-Jews are also circumcised. Therefore, circumcision does not necessarily distinguish Jews from non-Jews.

Alan Altmann, an uncircumcised son of Holocaust survivors, personally addresses the issue of circumcision and Jewish identity:

> Although uncircumcised, I am a very proud Jew, with a very strong sense of Jewish identity, and never hesitate to affirm my Jewish identity to Jew and non-Jew alike, but particularly to myself. I can assure you that having a foreskin has not made me less of a Jew than those without one, and in fact has given me additional reason to think about it.[6]

Is a man who is circumcised and is a member of a cult or commits immoral acts more of a Jew than an uncircumcised man who is committed to Jewish values and lives an ethical life? Is a circumcised atheist more of a Jew than an uncircumcised believer in one God? Clearly, being circumcised does not guarantee that one will be more religious or ethical.

Furthermore, there is no guarantee how or if an infant who is circumcised will practice Judaism when he grows up. This is true even among the Orthodox. According to the National Jewish Population Survey, 73 percent of Jews who were raised Orthodox did not call themselves Orthodox, and 29 percent of Jews raised Orthodox are now outside mainstream Judaism.[7] Should we be permanently altering the anatomy of our sons to comply with religious or cultural beliefs when we do not know whether our male children will grow up to accept or reject those beliefs?

Conformity

We can gain some insight into the behavior of Jews regarding circumcision by looking at group behavior in general. In all groups of people, there are expectations that group members will observe certain unspoken rules and standards of group behavior, also known as norms. Group norms tend to preserve the status quo. When a situation is ambiguous, group members' decisions are especially influenced by the group.[8] Group pressure can induce one person to harm another innocent perscn, and larger groups have greater influence over the behavior of individuals.[9] If one's behavior differs from group norms, there are four choices: conform, change the group norms, remain a deviant, or leave the group. In most cases, to minimize conflict and gain acceptance by others, people choose to conform.

Pressure on group members to conform increases when non-conformance is linked with the threat of a negative consequence. For example, believing that Jewish survival depends on circumcision would increase the pressure to conform. Stronger threats would further increase pressure to conform at the risk of reducing credibility, as in the rabbinic statement, "But for the blood of the covenant, heaven and earth would not endure" (Sab. 137b).

Many Jews are motivated to circumcise their sons because the practice gives us a sense of connection with other Jews. However, as with any practice, conforming without knowledge, understanding, and reflection tends to create a superficial type of connection. Many Jews do not learn about and understand circumcision and its effects, so it is not surprising that their scope of reflection is limited. (More than a few parents have told me that they questioned everything *except* circumcision.) Ties to the past are important, but we often equate the longevity of the practice with the depth of the connection to Judaism.

On a deeper, unconscious level, circumcision may actually inhibit connectedness. People who witness circumcision at the ritual often experience discomfort and anxiety, yet typically few express such feelings. Instead we sometimes disguise them with humor. In addition, the feelings of the infant, the one who is presumably being welcomed into the community, are generally ignored. Nobody responds to his cries while he is being held still for the procedure. Unrecognized and unexpressed anxiety about circumcision may limit the depth of our connection to each other (see also Chapters 6 and 7).

Health Claims

If the emotional and cultural reasons for circumcision are not convincing for some Jewish parents, health claims are frequently used to provide reassurance about the advisability of the practice. A summary of these claims is instructive. Currently the most widely used medical claim for circumcision is that it decreases the incidence of urinary tract infection (UTI) during the first year of life.[10] However, the UTI studies upon which this position is based have been criticized by some physicians, as well as by the American Academy of Pediatrics (AAP). The AAP concluded that the test designs and methods of these studies may have "flaws."[11] Another similar study found no confirmed cases of UTI in intact male infants without urinary birth defects.[12] Furthermore, using reduced UTI rates as a defense of circumcision is weak because the logic and reasoning leading to the conclusion are flawed.

1. Even according to the questionable studies, the overwhelming majority (at least 96–99 percent) of intact male infants do not get UTIs in the first year.[13] It is not reasonable to subject them to circumcision and the associated pain (see Chapter 3) without demonstrable benefit.

2. The studies do not consider the potential harm caused by circumcision. The rate of surgical complications is reported to be from 0.2 to 38 percent.[14] (The higher rate included complications reported during infants' first year.) There are at least twenty different complications including hemorrhage, infection, surgical injury, and in rare cases, death.[15] (Additional harm is discussed in Chapters 3 and 4.)

3. Circumcision involves cutting off normal, healthy, functioning tissue to prevent potential UTI problems in the future. There is no disease or infection present at the time of surgery. If we were to apply this principle in trying to prevent other potential problems, then we would be pulling healthy teeth to prevent cavities. Clearly, this principle is irrational.

4. UTI is treatable with antibiotics.[16] If good medical practice requires the least intrusive form of effective treatment, then circumcision is not justified, since it is a radical surgical treatment.

5. Female infants have a higher UTI rate than male infants,[17] yet no doctor advocates genital surgery to reduce female UTI.

Let's look at the validity of other medical claims, first generally and then individually. Most of the arguments that question the UTI claim would be applicable to *any* claimed medical benefit of circumcision. In addition, the AAP reports no *proven* benefit for circumcision after reviewing other medical claims. Regarding circumcision and penile cancer, they state, "Factors other than circumcision are important in the etiology of penile cancer. The incidence of penile cancer [1 in 100,000] is related to hygiene."[18]

The AAP also states, "Evidence regarding the relationship of circumcision to sexually transmitted diseases is conflicting. . . . Evidence linking uncircumcised men to cervical carcinoma is inconclusive." Regarding the cleanliness issue, the AAP reports: "The uncircumcised penis is easy to keep clean; no special care is required."[19] Normal bathing is sufficient. Since the incidence of a later medical need for circumcision in adulthood is as low as 6 in 100,000, circumcising an infant to prevent a later circumcision is unwarranted.[20]

Edward Wallerstein, who researched circumcision for twelve years, addressed the health issue in convincing detail in his book *Circumcision: An American Health Fallacy.* With approximately a thousand references to medical and associated literature around the world, Wallerstein found no health justification for routine circumcision.[21] Rosemary Romberg reached a similar conclusion after a thorough review in *Circumcision: The Painful Dilemma.*[22] Pediatrician Benjamin Spock reversed his original position in favor of circumcision and now writes: "I feel that there's no solid medical evidence at this time to support routine circumcision. . . . I recommend leaving the foreskin the way Nature meant it to be."[23]

Circumcision advocates, on the other hand, can only make the dubious claim that an unlikely or rare condition will be less likely to occur in the circumcised male. Many people accept this benefit as a justification for the procedure partly because circumcision is a surgical procedure that is done to *someone else.* Under such circumstances one is tempted to ask: Would you voluntarily submit to an unanesthetized surgical procedure on your healthy genitals for this "benefit"? Of course not. The answer is also evident from the fact that uncircumcised male adults rarely request to have themselves circumcised.

What is significant for this discussion is the frequency with which health claims are still used by Jews to support circumcision even though Wallerstein found that "there are no substantive data in Jewish circumcision history or practice to support the thesis that circumcision is a health measure or that health benefits are in any way derived from it. . . . Religious [traditional] Jews vehemently deny *any* health benefits and insist that circumcision is purely a religious rite."[24] Moreover, the eagerness to defend circumcision with health claims can result in the omission or misrepresentation of important information.

For example, a recent article in the Jewish press that defended circumcision with claimed health benefits was published in *Moment* magazine.[25] The article, written by the magazine's managing editor, contained many errors, omissions, and unsupported assertions in its coverage of recent medical research on circumcision.[26]

Particularly noteworthy was the omission of a sentence in a quote from the American Academy of Pediatrics 1989 Report of the Task Force on Circumcision referring to methodological flaws in certain studies claiming benefits of circumcision. Because of the deficiencies of these studies, the Task Force reported, the conclusions of these studies were tentative at best. Without this sentence the meaning of the quote from the Task Force changes and the Task Force appears to be more supportive of circumcision than was actually the case. Despite the fact that this and many other inaccuracies were called to the writer's attention prior to publication, the article was published unchanged.

Similarly, parents probably will not get a complete and accurate assessment of medical claims from a mohel (ritual circumciser; pl. mohelim). In the textbook of the Reform training program for mohelim, circumcision is promoted as a preventive measure against various diseases and infections.[27] Medical research that would dispute such assertions is not mentioned. The *Berit Milah Newsletter*, the publication of the same training program, also tends to be pro-circumcision on the topic of medical issues.

One of the reasons we hear about medical defenses for circumcision is that people want coherence and consistency among their beliefs. If inconsistency occurs a force then emerges to align beliefs.[28] Beliefs about medical benefits serve to support the common idea that circumcision is a good thing. However, in order to provide the medical rationales about circumcision, a few principles of logic and reason are violated, and some important factors (see Chapters 3 and 4) are ignored. The irrationality of the resulting position (e.g., item 3 in the UTI discussion) goes unrecognized by proponents of the practice. If circumcision were introduced today as a medical practice, it would have to be proven to be effective. This standard has not been met yet.

Jews who are aware of the lack of proven health benefits for circumcision may be more inclined to reexamine their motivation to circumcise.

3

Risks: Opinion versus Research

Pain

Let's review perceptions about the seriousness of circumcision pain as reported by various Jews connected with the practice. Rabbi and mohel Ronald Weiss comments on the degree of pain: "It's essentially as painless as you going to the barbershop to get your hair cut."[1] Expert mohel Romi Cohn, who has done thousands of circumcisions over the course of seventeen years, agrees that the procedure is "absolutely painless, for Jewish law is careful not to cause trauma to the child."[2] Rabbi Daniel Landes, who holds the University Chair in Jewish Ethics and Values at Yeshiva University in Los Angeles, and Sheryl Robbin, a writer with degrees in social work and human development, both equate the infant's experience of circumcision with receiving immunizations.[3] An article in the *Brit Milah Newsletter* suggests that placing a washcloth dipped in wine in the infant's mouth is sufficient because the pain is "mild," "easily tolerated, and quickly subsides . . . and the circumcision itself is less traumatic than being restrained."[4]

A respected Jewish psychologist and ritual circumciser has written,

> One can safely dispel the myth that infants are potentially traumatized by the circumcision, and can safely conclude that the circumcised infant experiences neither fear nor anxiety. The child certainly experiences brief, physical pain and discomfort but, being precognitive, when the pain ends it is as if the event never happened.[5]

A 1996 letter to the editor published in the *New York Times* by Rabbi Eugene Cohen, president of the Brith Milah Board of New York, reveals current Jewish thinking at a high level of authority. He states that newborns "cannot feel pain."[6]

An assistant professor of pediatrics at Boston University School of Medicine was "surprised" when he read Rabbi Cohen's letter and responded to the *New York Times* that recent studies "have dispelled this scientifically unfounded notion and demonstrated that the youngest infants do feel pain."[7] In a comprehensive review of recent medical literature on pain in newborns, investigators at Children's Hospital in Boston looked at anatomical, neurological, and neurochemical systems; cardiorespiratory, hormonal, and metabolic changes; body movement; facial expressions; crying; and complex behavioral responses such as temperament and sleep states. They concluded in an article published in the *New England Journal of Medicine* that newborn responses to pain are "similar to but greater than those observed in adult subjects."[8] This work is often cited in the medical literature whenever there is a discussion of infant pain, and its conclusions are now generally accepted by medical authorities.

The heart rate and blood pressure of newborn infants increase following a heel stick (a puncture to obtain a blood sample). Even infants born three months prematurely have physiological responses to the procedure.[9] The facial expressions of newborns responding to painful stimuli are similar to the facial expressions of adults responding to pain. Facial activity and cry pitch, intensity, and duration increase in infants if procedures are more invasive.[10]

When a heel stick is done to a newborn infant, the behavioral response is to withdraw the foot and cry. This response to pain is biological, not learned. The infant will even use the free foot to kick the doctor's hand away from the other foot. In a study using small electric shocks and pin pricks, some infants tried to use their hands to protect the area where they felt the pain.[11] In summary, the literature consistently supports the conclusion that infants feel, locate, and respond to painful stimuli. These findings have a direct bearing on the male infant's experience of circumcision.

To help in determining the degree of pain and stress caused by circumcision, infant response to circumcision was compared to that resulting from other procedures. Levels of cortisol (a hormone released into the blood in response to stress) and behavioral responses were recorded for newborns undergoing circumcision, heel-stick blood sampling, weighing and measuring, and discharge examination. Circumcision resulted in significantly higher levels of behavioral distress and blood cortisol levels as compared with the other procedures. Since the infant is restrained during circumcision, the response to the use of restraint was similarly tested and was not found to be measurably distressing to newborns.[12]

Circumcision is a surgical procedure that involves forcefully separating the foreskin from the glans (head of the penis) and then cutting it off. (Natural separation occurs with time. See Appendix F.) It is typically accomplished with a special clamp device (see Fig. 2 & 3). Over a dozen studies confirm the extreme pain associated with the procedure. It has been described as "among the most painful performed in neonatal medicine."[13] In one study researchers concluded that the pain was "severe and persistent."[14] Increases in heart rate of 55 beats per minute have been recorded, about a 50 percent increase over the baseline.[15] After circumcision, the level of blood cortisol had increased by a factor of three to four times the level measured prior to circumcision.[16] Investigators reported, "This level of pain would not be tolerated by older patients."[17]

Circumcision pain is described in a research study by Howard Stang and his colleagues from the Department of Pediatrics, Group Health Inc., and the University of Minnesota Institute of Child Development: "There is no doubt that circumcisions are painful for the baby. Indeed, circumcision has become a model for the analysis of pain and stress responses in the newborn." Stang and his associates report that the infant will "cry vigorously, tremble, and in some cases become mildly cyanotic [having blueness or lividness of the skin, caused by a deficiency of oxygen] because of prolonged crying."[18]

According to adult listeners in one study, the infant's response during circumcision included a cry that changed with the level of

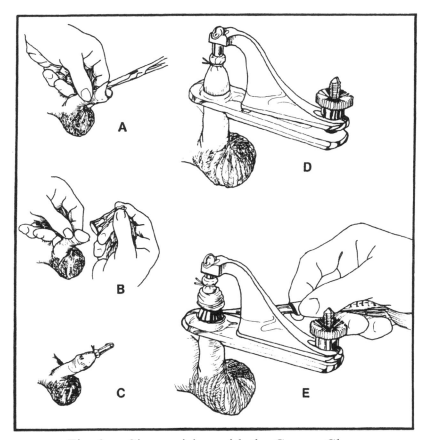

Fig. 2   Circumcision with the Gomco Clamp

The Gomco clamp is commonly used to perform circumcisions. It consists of three parts: a metal plate with a hole at one end, a round metal cap, and a screw device. The foreskin is first separated from the glans and cut lengthwise to expose the glans (A). Then the cap is placed over the glans (B). The foreskin is stretched up over the cap and tied securely to the cap handle (C). The hole at the end of the plate is placed over the cap and foreskin, and the flange on the handle is fitted into a groove in the screw device (D). Turning the screw device forces the cap against the hole and squeezes the foreskin. This squeezing prevents bleeding. Then the foreskin is cut off (E). The clamp remains in place at least five minutes to allow for clotting before it is removed.

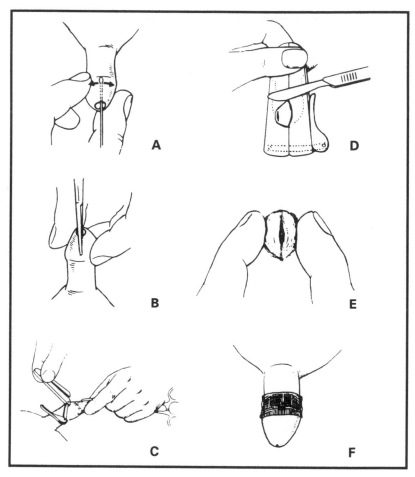

Fig. 3   Circumcision with the Mogen Clamp

The Mogen clamp is another commonly used circumcision device. The foreskin is separated from the glans with a probe (A). A hemostat is inserted to gauge and lock the amount of tissue to be cut off (B). The foreskin is drawn forward and placed into the jaws of the clamp (C). The hemostat is removed, the clamp is locked, and the foreskin is excised. The clamp is left on for one minute (D). The seal between the remaining shaft skin is broken, applying downward pressure until the glans is free (E). The penis is covered with a vaseline gauze (F).

pain being experienced. The most invasive part of the procedure caused the longest crying. These cries were high pitched and were judged most urgent.[19] A subsequent study confirmed that high-pitch cries were perceived to be more distressing and urgent.[20] Excessive crying can itself cause harm. In a rare case an infant undergoing circumcision cried vehemently for about ninety minutes and ruptured his stomach.[21]

The relationship between pain and vocal response needs clarification. Using a pacifier during circumcision reduces crying but does not affect hormonal pain response.[22] The effect of anesthetics given to the mother prior to birth also may reduce infant vocal responses. It takes more than a week for these anesthetics to leave the infant's body. Until that occurs, the newborn infant's vocal behavior is affected by them.[23] Therefore, the lack of crying can be explained, and other body signals demonstrate that the infant still experiences extreme pain during circumcision.

Other factors can also influence vocal behavior. Dr. Justin Call, an infant psychologist and professor-in-chief of child and adolescent psychology, University of California, Irvine, describes the infant's response to circumcision:

> The helpless, panicky cry of an infant when circumcised is an abnormal kind of cry. It is a breathless, high-pitched cry that is never heard in other normally occurring circumstances. Then sometimes babies who are being circumcised do exactly the opposite. They lapse into a semi-coma. Both of these states, helpless crying and semi-coma are abnormal states in the newborn.[24]

Tonya Brooks, midwife and president of the International Association for Childbirth at Home, writes, "In four of the nine circumcisions that I have seen, the baby didn't cry. He just seemed to be suddenly in a state of shock!"[25] Since the infant cannot escape physically, he attempts to escape psychologically by withdrawing from the overwhelming pain of the trauma. This explains why a crying infant may even stop crying during the cutting.[26]

During the Jewish ritual most people attempt to shield themselves from the infant's pain because it makes them uncomfortable. (In some cases people have fainted during the event.[27]) At the
bris I attended, the baby cried extremely hard for an extended
period (see Introduction). I later asked someone who was there
what she remembered about the infant's response. She said that
the baby did not cry at all!

A descriptive account of an infant's response to circumcision
pain is provided by Marilyn Milos, who witnessed a circumcision
during her training in nursing school:

> We students filed into the newborn nursery to find a baby strapped
> spread-eagle to a plastic board on a counter top across the room. He
> was struggling against his restraints—tugging, whimpering, and then
> crying helplessly. . . . I stroked his little head and spoke softly to him.
> He began to relax and was momentarily quiet. The silence was soon
> broken by a piercing scream—the baby's reaction to having his fore-
> skin pinched and crushed as the doctor attached the clamp to his pe-
> nis. The shriek intensified when the doctor inserted an instrument
> between the foreskin and the glans (head of the penis), tearing the
> two structures apart. The baby started shaking his head back and
> forth—the only part of his body free to move—as the doctor used
> another clamp to crush the foreskin lengthwise, which he then cut.
> This made the opening of the foreskin large enough to insert a cir-
> cumcision instrument, the device used to protect the glans from being
> severed during the surgery. The baby began to gasp and choke,
> breathless from his shrill continuous screams. . . . During the next
> stage of the surgery, the doctor crushed the foreskin against the cir-
> cumcision instrument and then, finally, amputated it. The baby was
> limp, exhausted, spent.[28]

Terry Schultz has worked in a hospital nursery. She wrote,

> When I have to set up for a circumcision, I feel like crying and often
> do. I feel like I'm betraying that being behind those eyes. . . . After
> witnessing many circumcisions, I can say: Yes, it hurts. It's pure and
> simple torture. As often as I can, I leave the room for the slaughter. I
> just can't bear to watch another. . . . More than the cry, it's the look

in those trusting eyes as it all begins (before they are squeezed closed in terror).[29]

There is disagreement among physicians about using anesthesia during circumcisions. Because no experimental anesthetic has been found to be safe and effective in *preventing* circumcision pain, research in this area continues. A local injection, the best option tested, reduces circumcision pain but still is not typically administered due to a lack of familiarity with its use, as well as the belief that it introduces additional risk.[30] Although there are indications that the risk is minimal, most physicians who perform circumcisions do not use anesthetics even after they are taught how. When an anesthetic is used, its effect wears off before the post-operative pain does.[31] Meanwhile, some physicians have taken a strong stand on the issue of using anesthesia during circumcision. For instance, in a recent medical article on the subject, Drs. Rabinowitz and Hulbert described circumcision without pain relief as "barbaric."[32] Pediatrician Neil Schechter wrote that subjecting an adult to the same practice would be "unfathomable."[33]

Some Jews believe, without any specific knowledge or evidence, that the circumcision methods of mohelim are superior to those of doctors and cause less pain to the infant. Actually, traditional mohel methods have included using sharp fingernails for cutting.[34] Sucking blood from the cut by mouth and spitting it into a container has been done "throughout the ages."[35] Both practices were generally abandoned at the end of the nineteenth century but are still used in some communities.[36]

Today most mohelim get their training in hospitals and many are also doctors. The recently organized training programs for both Reform and Conservative mohelim require a valid medical license for certification. In the last century, modern clamp devices have been adopted by mohelim as well as doctors, but most Orthodox mohelim do not use clamp devices because they believe bleeding is a religious requirement. Infants circumcised without clamp devices are more at risk of hemorrhaging. To the extent that mohelim and doctors use the same device, the pain experienced by the infant would be the same. In addition, the typical circumcision requires the forceful separation of the foreskin from the glans (see Figs. 2 & 3), a process that, according to studies of infants' cries during circumcision, is associated with maximum pain response.[37] Since both mohelim and doctors must separate the foreskin from the glans before cutting it off, the pain experienced by infants would be comparable.

Behavioral Changes Following Circumcision

Beginning in the 1970s some studies investigated the effect of circumcision on infant behavior. Researchers found differences in sleep patterns and increased irritability among circumcised infants.[38] In addition, changes in infant-maternal interaction were observed over the course of the first twenty-four hours after circumcision.[39] For example, breast- and bottle-fed infants' feeding behavior has been shown to deteriorate after circumcision.[40] Other behavior differences have been noted on the day following the procedure.[41] The American Academy of Pediatrics (AAP) Task Force on Circumcision noted these behavioral changes resulting from circumcision in their report.[42]

In one study researchers stated that European reports of newborn infant responses to hearing and taste stimulation showed little difference in responses between males and females, but related tests on American infants showed significant gender differences. Investigators suggested that these differences could be the result of circumcision and not gender. They concluded that circumcision "may have long-term physiological and behavioral consequences."[43]

In one of the most important studies, researchers observed that the behavior of nearly 90 percent of circumcised infants significantly changed after the circumcision.[44] Some became more active, and some became less active. The quality of the change generally was associated with whether they were crying or quiet respectively at the start of the circumcision. This result suggests that infants use different coping styles when they are subjected to extreme pain. In addition, the researchers observed that infants who had been circumcised were less able to comfort themselves or to be comforted by others.

Some mothers and nurses who have contacted the Circumcision Resource Center also reported behavior changes in circumcised infants. Some of these changes are caused by the extreme sensitivity of the fresh wound left by circumcision. Sally Hughes, an obstetrical nurse who has seen many circumcised infants before they go home, reported,

> When you lay them on their stomachs they scream. When their diaper is wet they scream. Normally, they don't scream if their diaper is wet. Baby boys who are not circumcised do not scream like that. The circumcised babies are more irritable, and they nurse poorly.[45]

Mothers reported that their infants changed temperament after the circumcision, cried for extended periods at home, and seemed inconsolable.

Researchers at Children's Hospital in Boston noted changes in sleep patterns, activity level, irritability, and mother-infant interaction among circumcised infants. They concluded,

> The persistence of specific behavioral changes after circumcision in neonates implies the presence of memory. In the short term, these behavioral changes may disrupt the adaptation of newborn infants to their postnatal environment, the development of parent-infant bonding, and feeding schedules.[46]

Circumcision may even permanently alter the structure and function of developing neural pathways, which could have an impact on future responses to pain.[47] This is supported by a study of the impact of circumcision four to six months after the event. Canadian investigators reported that during vaccinations circumcised boys had increased behavioral pain response and cried for significantly longer periods than did uncircumcised boys. The researchers noted that circumcision, like any unanesthetized surgery, could result in post-traumatic stress disorder. The increased pain response at vaccination could be due to reliving the earlier traumatic experience.[48]

Trauma

The extreme pain of circumcision, behavioral changes following the procedure, and the Canadian study raise the serious question of trauma. The *Diagnostic and Statistical Manual of Mental Disorders (DSM-IV)*, published by the American Psychiatric Association and the bible of mental health clinicians and researchers, is helpful in responding to this question. Its description of a traumatic event includes an event that is beyond usual human experience, such as assault (sexual or physical), torture, and a threat to one's physical integrity.[49] An assault is a physical attack. Torture is severe pain or anguish. It does not necessarily take account of intention or purpose but focuses on the act itself and the experience of the victim.

From the perspective of the infant, all the elements in this *DSM-IV* description of traumatic events apply to circumcision of a male infant: the procedure involves being forcibly restrained, having part of the penis cut off, and experiencing extreme pain. Based on the nature of the experience and considering the extreme physiological and behavioral responses of the infant, circumcision traumatizes the infant.

The question of an infant's capacity to experience trauma needs to be emphasized. John Wilson, an author with a national reputation for trauma research, supports the view that effects of trauma can occur "at any point in the life cycle, from infancy and childhood to the waning years of life."[50] In addition, the *DSM-IV* states that traumatic effects "can occur at any age."[51]

It is reasonable to expect that virtually all organisms have a limit to the degree and type of stressful and painful experience they can assimilate. Exposure to such experience beyond that limit results in trauma. Based on many research studies of circumcised infants, circumcision exceeds that limit.

Complications

Whether an infant is circumcised in the hospital by medical staff or in the home by a mohel, there are medical risks as with any surgery. This element of risk occurs to Rabbi Schachter-Shalomi: "What if the knife slips?"[52] As mentioned in the last chapter, the rate of surgical complications is reported to be from 0.2 to 38 percent.[53] (The higher rate included complications reported during the infants' first year.) There are at least twenty different complications including hemorrhage, infection, and surgical injury. On rare occasions death has resulted.[54] For this reason traditional Jewish law allows for exemptions when other children in a family have died from the effects of circumcision. If two brothers have died from complications resulting from circumcision, subsequent male infants must not be operated on until they are older and better able to tolerate the operation. If two sisters lose a son due to complications from circumcision, other sisters shall not have their sons circumcised.[55]

Awareness of complications resulting from ritual circumcision is low because such instances are rarely reported unless the infant requires hospitalization, the family sues, or the infant dies. Mohelim may be certified, but there is little supervision of their practice. They do most circumcisions in private homes, and because they are not required to keep records, complications are not documented. Even in hospitals there is a lack of recording and reporting of circumcision complications.

Based on the latest research studies, the effects of circumcision on the infant are much greater than are generally assumed. The infant's pain is extreme, behavioral changes have an unknown duration, and, according to recognized criteria, circumcision is traumatic. In addition, the risk of complications deserves consideration. If circumcision were introduced today as a medical practice, it would have to be proven to be safe, a standard that has not been met. These factors alone should be sufficient to give parents reason to carefully evaluate the advisability of circumcision for their son. But there are reports of other effects as well. The evidence of long-term effects of circumcision on adults is discussed in the next chapter.

4

Unrecognized Consequences

Sexual Impact

Advocates of circumcision either do not recognize the sexual impact of circumcision, or judge that the altered state constitutes an improvement. For example, Rabbi Daniel Landes of Yeshiva University and freelance writer Sheryl Robbin defend circumcision by stating that "the male is not considered perfect at birth."[1] Reflecting the views expressed in ancient rabbinic texts, they say that the male's sexual drive is inherently "evil" and requires "restraint." Circumcision serves as a "repair of nature." Similar ideas are expressed repeatedly by Rabbi Paysach Krohn, a fifth-generation mohel, in his book *Bris Milah*.[2] An early rabbinic belief was that with reduced sexual activity, a circumcised man could more easily concentrate on study of the Torah.[3]

The *Encyclopedia Judaica* also expresses a negative attitude toward male sexuality. "It [circumcision] sanctified the human body and aided it in its fight against erotic indulgence."[4] The first-century Jewish philosopher Philo similarly defended circumcision by claiming that it "represents the excision of the pleasure of sex, which bewitches the mind."[5] Recounting his anxious experience in making the circumcision decision for his own son, Rabbi Schachter-Shalomi wonders if "something destructive and 'macho' gets refined by a Bris."[6] Moses Maimonides, the renowned physician, philosopher, rabbi, and scholar, believed that limiting sexual intercourse had moral value. He wrote in 1190 that the object of circumcision was to weaken the organ of generation as far as possible, and thus cause man to be moderate. . . . Circumcision weakens the power of sexual excitement, and sometimes lessens the natural enjoyment.[7]

Contemporary research supports the ancient notion that circumcision diminishes sexual pleasure. In order to appreciate the sexual functions of the foreskin, refer to Figures 4–8, which clarify what the foreskin is and how it works. Figures 4 and 5 show the difference between a circumcised and a natural penis in the relaxed or flaccid state. Note that the foreskin serves to cover the glans or head of the penis. Figure 6 shows this diagrammatically. Figure 7 shows the circumcised penis in the erect state. The shaft skin is taut. Figure 8 shows beginning, continuing, and complete erection of the natural penis. Note that the inner foreskin layer becomes exposed and the entire foreskin moves to loosely cover the penile shaft.

Taylor, Lockwood, and Taylor studied foreskin tissue at the Department of Pathology, Health Sciences Centre, University of Manitoba, Canada, and reported their results in the *British Journal of Urology* in an article titled "The Prepuce: Specialized Mucosa of the Penis and Its Loss to Circumcision." Based on the examination of 22 adult foreskins obtained at autopsy, they found that the outer foreskin's concentration of nerves is "impressive," and its "sensitivity to light touch and pain are similar to that of the skin of the penis as a whole."[8] The foreskin inner surface is different. It is mucous membrane similar to the inner surface of the mouth, also rich in nerves and blood vessels. Between the inner and outer layers of the foreskin is a unique structure they call a "ridged band" that contains "specialized nerve endings."[9] The researchers concluded that the foreskin has several kinds of nerves and "should be considered a structural and functional unit made up of more or less specialized parts. . . . The glans and penile shaft gain excellent if surrogate sensitivity from the prepuce [foreskin]."[10]

The foreskin represents at least a third of the penile skin. It protects the glans from abrasion and contact with clothes.[11] The foreskin also increases sexual pleasure by sliding up and down on

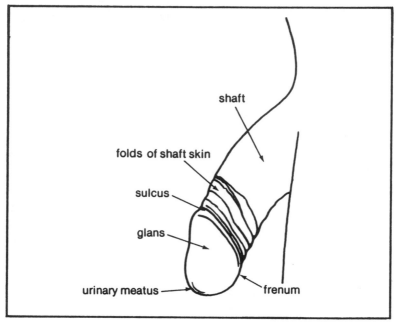

Fig. 4   Circumcised Penis in the Relaxed State

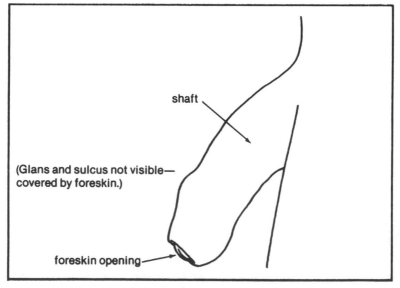

Fig. 5   Natural Penis in the Relaxed State

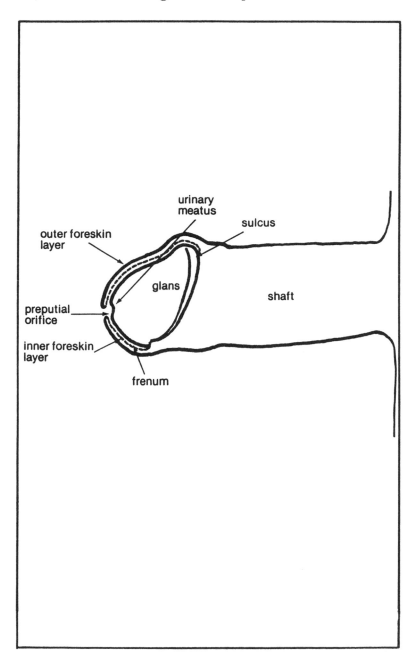

Fig. 6   Inner and Outer Foreskin Layers

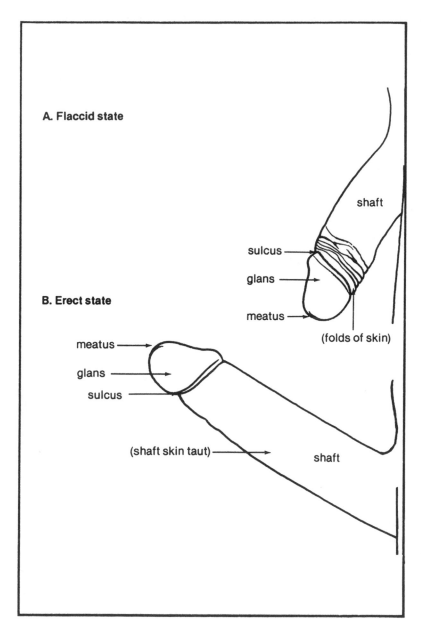

Fig. 7   Erectile Process in the Circumcised Penis

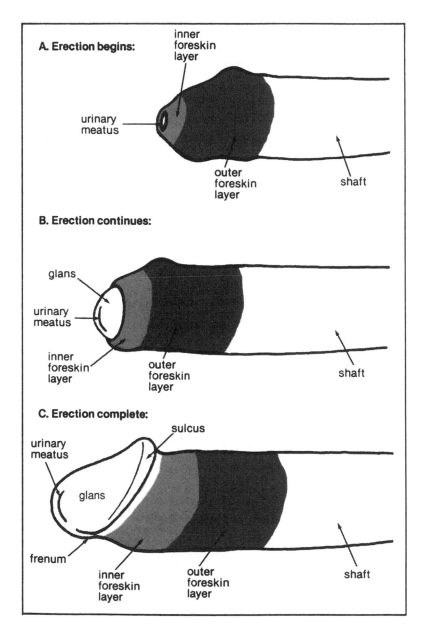

Fig. 8   Erectile Process in the Natural Penis

the shaft, stimulating the glans by alternately covering and exposing it. This can occur during masturbation or intercourse. Because of this moveable skin, friction is minimized. In addition, a secretion called smegma of the inner foreskin layer provides natural lubrication and helps to keep the glans surface smooth and soft.[12] On the circumcised penis, the glans skin, which would be moist mucous membrane if it were protected by the foreskin, becomes dry and thickens considerably over time. As a result it is less sensitive than the glans of a natural penis.[13] Supplementary lubrication is sometimes needed to facilitate masturbation and intercourse for the circumcised penis.

Only men circumcised as adults can experience the difference a foreskin makes. In the *Journal of Sex Research*, Money and Davison from the Johns Hopkins University School of Medicine reported on five such men. Changes included diminished penile sensitivity and gratification. The investigators concluded,

> Erotosexually and cosmetically, the operation is, for the most part, contraindicated, and it should be evaluated in terms of possible pathological sequelae.[14]

Other men circumcised as adults regret the change.

> Slowly the area lost its sensitivity, and as it did, I realized I had lost something rather vital. Stimuli that had previously aroused ecstasy had relatively little effect. . . . Circumcision destroys a very joyful aspect of the human experience for males and females.[15]

> After the circumcision there was a major change. It was like night and day. I lost most sensation. I would give anything to get the feeling back. I would give my house. [This man's physician persuaded him to be circumcised by warning him that otherwise he was at risk of getting penile cancer. When the man complained of the result, the physician replied, "That's normal."][16]

> The greatest disadvantage of circumcision is the awful loss of sensitivity when the foreskin is removed. . . . On a scale of ten, the intact penis experiences pleasure that is at least eleven or twelve; the circumcised penis is lucky to get to three.[17]

After thirty years in the natural state I allowed myself to be persuaded by a physician to have the foreskin removed—not because of any problems at the time, but because, in the physician's view, there might be problems in the future. That was five years ago and I am sorry I had it done. . . . The sensitivity in the glans has been reduced by at least 50 percent. There it is, unprotected, constantly rubbing against the fabric of whatever I am wearing. In a sense, it has become callused.[18]

The sexual differences between a circumcised and uncircumcised penis is . . . like wearing a condom or wearing a glove. . . . Sight without color would be a good analogy. . . . Only being able to see in black-and-white, for example, rather than seeing in full color would be like experiencing an orgasm with a foreskin and without. There are feelings you'll just never have without a foreskin.[19]

As more information is disclosed, an increasing number of men are distressed about the sexual impact of circumcision. Writer Richard Newman speaks for many men when he concludes, "Circumcised men have lost, have had stolen from us, not only a highly sensitive and extremely functional part of our bodies, but also part of the full sexuality that ought to have been ours."[20]

Psychological Effects

Because of the atmosphere of denial surrounding the issue, there are no published formal studies of the long-term psychological effects of circumcision. However, there are signs that such effects exist in at least some men. The Circumcision Resource Center and several other organizations that educate the public about circumcision are receiving a growing number of letters from men all around the country expressing dissatisfaction with their circumcision. Following are some statements excerpted from letters received at the Circumcision Resource Center:

Circumcision has given my life a much diminished and shameful flavor.

My penis feels incomplete, deformed, maimed.

Being circumcised has ruined my sex life.

I have felt a deep rage for a long time about this.

I've always felt I'm missing normal male experience, and I'm embarrassed when in public dressing rooms.

I feel violated and abused.

I have felt unhappy about it all my life.

I am very angry and resentful about this. I've had many physical, psychological, and emotional problems all my life.

No one had the right to cut my foreskin off!

I feel cheated at having been robbed of what is my natural birthright.

I never mentioned it to my parents.

The single most traumatic event of my life with the greatest psychological damage was my circumcision as an infant.

The written and oral responses of men dissatisfied with their circumcision tend to include at least one of the following feelings:

    anger, resentment, revenge, rage, hate
    sense of loss, deficiency, diminished body image
    disbelief, lack of understanding, confusion
    embarrassment, shame
    sense of having been victimized, cheated, robbed, raped,
        violated, abused, mutilated, deformed
    fear, distrust, withdrawal
    grief, sadness, pain
    envy of intact men

Similar feelings were reported in a preliminary survey in which over 300 self-selected circumcised men responded to a request to document the harmful effects of their circumcision.[21]

Over 80 percent of respondents cited emotional harm. Moreover, in a recent issue of a major medical journal, twenty men signed a letter saying, "We are all adult men who believe that we have been harmed by circumcision."[22] These reports do not tell us how widespread the discontent is, but *that these feelings are being expressed at all is a noteworthy development and reason for concern.*

Reports of negative reactions to circumcision are surprising to those who assume that circumcision is a benign procedure. How can we reconcile the existence of such reports with the fact that the majority of circumcised men do not express these feelings about their circumcision? The following factors reduce the likelihood that circumcised men will express dissatisfaction with their circumcision:

1. Accepting American circumcision beliefs and cultural assumptions prevents men from recognizing and feeling their dissatisfaction. A typical response is "When I was young I was told it was necessary for health reasons. I guess I just didn't question that. I assumed that was so."
2. The emotions about circumcision that may surface are very painful. Repressing them protects men from experiencing pain. A circumcised man recalled, "It was something I just didn't examine. I put it away in the back of my mind like a lot of guys do." If the feelings do become conscious, they can still be suppressed. After learning about circumcision, another man said, "I don't want to be angry about this."
3. Those who have feelings about their circumcision are generally afraid to express them because they are afraid that their feelings may be dismissed or ridiculed. When asked why he had not revealed his feelings about circumcision before, one man said, "I would be looked upon as strange or else people would toss it off lightly." Another said, "It's not something that anyone talks about. If it is talked about, it's in a snickering, comical way which I find disturbing. People laugh about it as if there is something funny going on."

4. Verbal expression of feelings requires conscious awareness. Because early traumas are generally unconscious, associated feelings are expressed nonverbally through behavioral, emotional, and physiological reactions.[23] Attitudes about people, life, and the future may also be affected. An example of an attitude resulting from childhood trauma is "You can't count on anything or anyone to protect you."[24]

Lack of awareness and understanding of circumcision, emotional repression, fear of disclosure, and nonverbal expression help keep feelings about circumcision a secret.

The overwhelming majority of circumcised men were circumcised as newborn infants. The memory of this event is not in their conscious awareness. Consequently, the connection between present feelings and circumcision may not be clear. For example, a circumcised man wondering about the effects of being circumcised said,

> It seems to me that there's got to be a connection between circumcision and how I feel about my genitals and my sexuality. It just isn't reasonable to me that there wouldn't be a connection there. I think it's something that's so deeply buried that it's going to take more exploration on my part for me to get in touch with it. It's pretty disturbing that circumcision was the first sexual experience that I ever had.

The men quoted earlier attribute many negative feelings to their circumcision. Is this an accurate connection to make, and how did it originate? I explored this question by asking men who contacted the Circumcision Resource Center when and how they first recognized their feelings about circumcision. Based on their responses, the answer lies in the impact of discovering one's circumcision as a child. If a child grows up in a community that has children of differing circumcision status, it is probable that the day will come when a circumcised boy will notice the difference. Under certain circumstances, this realization can have traumalike consequences such as recurrent unwelcome thoughts and images.

One man told of an indelible scene when he was four. He was with an intact boy who showed him his penis and explained circumcision to him. He was shocked and ashamed at what had been done to him and thought, "Why would somebody want to do that to me? They just chopped it off. It didn't make any sense to me." As an adult he thinks about it "every time I take a shower or urinate."

The man who stated earlier in this chapter that his circumcision was "the single most traumatic event of my life" related this experience:

> My initial awareness came when I was about five years old and playing with the boy who lived down the street. I discovered that he had that skin and I didn't. I don't remember anything in terms of verbal exchange. It's now sixty years later, and the memory is still very vivid, the two of us sitting on his bathroom floor. It had a profound effect, an imprinting on my mind. Then, when I was about thirteen, I went swimming with a friend at one of the local lakes. When we were changing into bathing suits, I realized that he was uncircumcised. That, again, was a strong imprint. Probably those two early experiences were enough to create a very strong picture in my mind and cause a realization of my loss. I had no idea at the time of how traumatic it was. I only knew that there was something different, and I was thinking about it so much every day.

Another man remembered his childhood discovery:

> I've been angry about being circumcised since I was six years old. I was taking a hike in the woods with my older brother and his friend. We all had to use the tree. My brother said to his friend, "What's wrong with you?" His friend said, "It's not what's wrong with me. It's you guys." His mother was a nurse, and she knew better than to do it to him. We didn't know the terminology. We didn't understand it, but he told us that we were born the way he was, and then someone cut part of us off. I haven't talked to my brother about it over the years, but all my life I've been just dying for the chance to get my hands on the doctor that did it to me.

The following story is typical:

The shock and surprise of my life came when I was in junior high school, and I was in the showers after gym. . . . I wondered what was wrong with those penises that looked different than mine. . . . I soon realized I had part of me removed. I felt incomplete and very frustrated when I realized that I could never be like I was when I was born—intact. That frustration is with me to this day. Throughout life I have regretted my circumcision. Daily I wish I were whole.

A man who first recognized his dissatisfaction with circumcision as an adult reported:

What changed my feeling about circumcision was recognizing that this was done to me without my consent at a time when I couldn't do anything to stop it. I don't see anything wrong with having the option. I just don't like the idea that someone made this decision for me. I'll never know how it feels to be uncircumcised.

5

Personal Experiences

With so many factors to consider, no wonder some Jewish parents are carefully evaluating the advisability of circumcision before making a decision. Rabbis are receiving a growing number of calls about circumcision from parents in conflict.[1] Michael Meyer, author and professor of Jewish history, also finds "an increasing number of Reform Jewish parents, including some very Jewishly committed ones, now express hesitation about circumcising their sons."[2]

Rabbi Schachter-Shalomi, a Jewish renewal teacher and writer, acknowledges the conflict experienced by Jewish parents, presumably feelings that many of them have expressed to him over the years. To the new parent he says,

> You wish you did not have to take your baby, a new person who loves and trusts you, and inflict the trauma of an operation on him. Yes, inflict is the word, let's not make it pretty.[3]

Referring to community pressure to perform the "brutal procedure," Schachter-Shalomi concludes, "It is a gut-wrenching experience" for all Jewish parents.[4] (He also feels that circumcision "connects us with others" and supports Jewish survival.[5]) One mother wrote, "I spent most of my pregnancy crying, vomiting, ruminating, and reading about circumcision."[6] Pregnant mothers sometimes reveal that they hope for a girl so that they can avoid circumcision.

Parents Who Circumcised Their Son

In many cases, parents feel resigned to the fact that their son will be circumcised. Most Jews have their son circumcised in a hospital where it is done in a special room away from the parents, yet many Jewish circumcisions are done in the home of the parents in a ritual attended by family and friends. Although some parents may report that the occasion is a positive experience, it is not always the case. According to a study on adult responses to infant crying, women are more likely than men to report feeling distressed.[7] Witnessing the circumcision and the infant's response can have a particularly shocking effect on the mother.

Only recently have some parents been willing to describe their agonizingly painful experiences at their son's circumcision. Because these experiences are not usually shared, it is important to give them particular attention. They give us a new perspective to add to what we already know. Though further research is needed to reveal how common such experiences are, the fact that people have expressed these troubled feelings is reason for concern and reflection.

Some mothers have written about their experiences with circumcision during the previous year. One related this memory:

> My tiny son and I sobbed our hearts out. . . . After everything I'd worked for, carrying and nurturing Joseph in the womb, having him at home against no small odds, keeping him by my side constantly since birth, nursing him whenever he needed closeness and nourishment—the circumcision was a horrible violation of all I felt we shared. I cried for days afterward.[8]

Another mother noted that she still felt pain recalling the experience about a year later. She wrote to her son:

> I have never heard such screams. . . . Will I ever know what scars this brings to your soul? . . . What is that new look I see in your eyes? I can see pain, a certain sadness, and a loss of trust.[9]

Other mothers clearly remember their son's circumcision after many years. Miriam Pollack reported over a dozen years later,

"The screams of my babies remain embedded in my bones and still haunt the edges of my mind." She told me the cry of one son "sounded like he was being butchered. I lost my milk."[10]

Nancy Wainer Cohen recalled her feelings connected with the circumcision of her son, who is now twenty-two:

> I heard him cry during the time they were circumcising him. The thing that is most disturbing to me is that I can still hear his cry. . . . I will go to my grave hearing that horrible wail and feeling somewhat responsible, feeling that it was my lack of awareness, my lack of consciousness. I did the best I could, and it wasn't good enough.[11]

Two other mothers have reported to the Circumcision Resource Center that witnessing the pain of their son's circumcision was "the worst day of my life."

Elizabeth Pickard-Ginsburg vividly remembered her son's circumcision and its effect on her:

> Jesse was shrieking and I had tears streaming down my face. . . . He was screaming and there was no doubt in his scream that he wanted mother, or a mothering figure to come and protect him from this pain!! . . . Jesse screamed so loud that all of a sudden there was no sound! I've never heard anything like it!! He was screaming and it went up and then there was no sound and his mouth was just open and his face was full of pain!! I remember something happened inside me . . . the intensity of it was like blowing a fuse! It was too much. We knew something was over. I don't feel that it ever really healed. . . . I don't think I can recover from it. It's a scar. I've put a lot of energy into trying to recover. I did some crying and we did some therapy. There's still a lot of feeling that's blocked off. It was too intense. . . . We had this beautiful baby boy and seven beautiful days and this beautiful rhythm starting, and it was like something had been shattered!! . . . When he was first born there was a tie with my young one, my newborn. And when the circumcision happened, in order to allow it *I had cut off the bond.* I had to cut off my natural instincts, and in doing so *I cut off a lot of feelings towards Jesse.* I cut it off to repress the pain and to repress the natural instinct to stop the circumcision.[12]
> (italics added)

After several years, Pickard-Ginsburg says she can still feel "an element of detachment" toward her son. Her account is particularly revealing. Having "cut off" feelings toward her son by observing and not interfering with his circumcision had a lasting effect on her relationship with her son.

Observing their son's circumcision has left some parents with a deep feeling of regret. The following quotes are typical:

> I am so sorry I was so ignorant about circumcision. Had I witnessed a circumcision first, I never would have consented to having my son circumcised.[13]

> Always in the back of my mind I've thought, "I wish he hadn't been cut." I have apologized to him numerous times.[14]

> If I had ever known, I wouldn't have done this in a million years. I don't care what my religion is.[15]

Observing a son's circumcision can have a physical effect.

> I felt as if I might pass out at the sight of my son lying there, unable to move or defend himself. His screams tore at my heart as his fore-skin was heartlessly torn from his penis. Too late to turn back, I knew that this was a terrible mistake and that it was something that no one, especially newborn babies, should ever have to endure. A wave of shock coursed through me—my body feeling nauseatingly sick with guilt and shame. All I could think of was holding and con-soling my child, but his pain felt inconsolable—his body rigid with fear and anger—his eyes filled with tears of betrayal.[16]

A father also wrote of betrayal:

> My son screamed. Unmistakable screams of pain. Sounds I'd never heard from him before. I felt a wave of sickness come over me. It wasn't a physical nausea. It was something much deeper. A horror. How could I allow this to happen to him? . . . I was in a state of shock. . . . I found tears rolling down my face. I had betrayed my son. I had betrayed myself. . . . For a long time after the wound healed, my son seemed a different person, quick to cry, slow to calm.[17]

Even if a mother does not observe her son's circumcision, she must look at his wounded* penis every time she changes his diaper. One mother reported, "Every time I changed his diaper I cried. It was so red and raw." Another mother recalled, "His penis was red for so long. It just looked horrible to me." Do these maternal feelings toward the infant son's penis have an effect on the infant?

It is natural for human beings to experience guilt when we have harmed another person or violated some rule. The Circumcision Resource Center has received letters from mothers who feel a deep sense of guilt for having allowed their sons to be circumcised. In the words of one mother, "I have a lot of stuff going on about not having stood up for something that I knew intuitively was the wrong thing to do." A mother of three sons related this story:

> The first one, I didn't know, but I should have educated myself. The second one, I should have insisted on no circumcision. The third one, I insisted. It was as easy as that.

The mother of a four-year-old boy wrote,

> There is a deep wound of guilt in my heart around my son's circumcision. Though not the only mistake I made in parenting, it is certainly the gravest and the one I have the most trouble forgiving myself for. . . . I've cried many times about my son's circumcision. Somehow I keep thinking I should have known better. How can I forgive myself for this one? And how can my son forgive me? How can I make it up to him? . . . I just now realized that my son's circumcision wounded me as well as him. I carry his pain as well as my guilt.[18]

Other parents may not express strong adverse reactions to a son's circumcision, possibly for two reasons. First, because the feelings engendered by circumcision are so painful and are not generally supported by the community, they may be suppressed. One regretful

---

* After the skin of the penis is cut and removed, there is a wound. Once the wound has healed, a scar remains. Most circumcised men are not aware of their circumcision scar.

mother said, "I honestly believe that women have to numb out and anesthetize themselves in order to allow this to happen."[19] Second, as described earlier, if the infant goes into traumatic shock, he does not cry, and parents tend to interpret lack of crying as a sign that circumcision is not painful. Some parents and guests at a bris even experience a feeling of relief if the infant does not cry. People who challenge these explanations have the burden of accounting for the distress of some parents of circumcised sons.

The feelings that some parents have about observing their son's circumcision are rarely heard by rabbis. Miriam Pollack, a mother who regrets the circumcision of her son, has had close religious, social, political, and professional connections to Jewish life. She explains,

> At the time of my son's circumcision I was not aware of the validity of my feelings. My trauma was so profound I couldn't talk about it. I felt paralyzed. When I learned the facts about circumcision nine years later, I realized that my maternal intuition was grounded in wisdom. I found my voice. I have been listening to rabbis all my life, but a rabbi is not someone I would talk to about this. I know what they would say. I don't want to hear them attempt to justify circumcision.[20]

The strong emotional responses of some mothers to circumcision raise the question of what possible effects their feelings have on their behavior toward their sons. For example, mothers could exhibit overprotectiveness associated with guilt, or withdrawal connected with their own pain.

Whether they witness the procedure or not, mothers who consent to circumcision are often left wondering what impact it may have on their son. As the child grows up, some mothers ask themselves, "Why is my son distant from me?" Based on the accounts in this chapter, perhaps it is time to investigate whether circumcision is part of the answer to this question.

Parents Who Did Not Circumcise

Over twenty-five years ago the *Encyclopedia Judaica* acknowledged that some Reform Jews choose not to have their sons circumcised.[21] Today an increasing number of Jewish parents are finding the courage to say no to circumcision. At the Circumcision Resource Center, we have heard from hundreds of Jews who either have not circumcised their son, or would not circumcise a future son. One parent who did not circumcise, a member of a Conservative congregation, is mentioned in an article in *Jewish Monthly*. The article also quotes a rabbi who reports, "It's usually done [forgoing circumcision] by the few who are intellectually alert and do not take things for granted."[22]

Natalie Bivas decided against circumcision for her son. She had attended a bris three years earlier. "The baby was livid and shrieking for a full twenty-minutes. . . . My husband fainted, and I sobbed uncontrollably."[23] In explaining her decision to her parents in a letter, Bivas concluded,

> One thing is certain: if we allowed our infant son to be tied down and approached with a knife, we would die a thousand deaths in our hearts and souls. . . . We certainly cannot watch him suffer for no good reason.[24]

A Jewish mother who did not circumcise her five-month-old boy had the calm conviction to handle her family's reaction.

> Half-jokingly, my mother did say to me at one point, "I've tried everything else. I'm going to try emotional blackmail. You wouldn't want to hurt your father and me." And I said, "I would do anything not to hurt you, my parents, except hurt my child."[25]

Alan Shulman also said no to circumcision. He simply trusted his feelings. He said that the decision not to circumcise his son was

> a relatively easy one for me. I found that witnessing the circumcision of my cousin's son a few years earlier was a viscerally painful and unpleasant experience. I felt some anxiety about going against the traditions of my upbringing, but the practice of circumcision is really a barbaric act. Circumcision is a mutilation that is not justified by any tradition, any ritual. It deprives the male child of something that is rightfully his.[26]

Jim Paisner, the father of two intact sons in their twenties, explains,

> The male human was not born that way [circumcised]. Is there any reason to think that this is some kind of improvement on the way humans have been born for a million years? That was the kind of approach that we took to it.[27]

In a letter to the editor of the *New York Times Book Review*, Ralph Ginzburg expressed a similar view about the practice of circumcision in America: "Is it really credible that over half of American baby boys who come into this world are born defective and must be 'fixed'?"[28]

Moshe Rothenberg, an observant Jew, reported his experience: "I have been to a number of brises. At none of them did a single person note the pain that every eight-day-old boy was expressing." Rothenberg decided before the birth of his own son, who is now nine years old, not to circumcise him.

> We have a higher level of awareness than people in the Bible. . . . I don't believe in sacrifice. . . . I fell in love with my son the first seven days. There was no way we were going to hurt him. . . . We got respect for putting our values into practice.[29]

"Something Just Came Over Me"

The decision process of Dana and David Parmes-Katz was particularly eventful.[30] Dana called the Circumcision Resource Center recently to describe her situation. She and her husband were both nonobservant, reformist Jews. She was expecting a boy in several weeks and was opposed to circumcising him. Her husband wanted the circumcision. She said of her husband,

> He's never done anything traditional in his life, and all of a sudden he wants to be traditional. He's really stuck on this. He says he's not giving in. . . . He believes it's something you have to do as a Jew.

Her husband, David, said, "I just felt that I wanted to circumcise. I don't know what reason. It's just the type of thing you are supposed to do."

Three weeks went by, and Dana and David had made no progress toward resolving the disagreement. The subject was so emotional that they only talked about it at specific times. The baby was due in another three weeks.

The next month Dana called to tell the rest of her story:

We had decided to do it. I was crying every day. I was so upset. I couldn't believe I was doing this. Then something just came over me. I went with my gut and realized I couldn't go through with it. I became like a mother lion protecting her cub. I had to tell him, and I just poured my heart out to him. Wednesday night before the circumcision I said, "I can't do this tomorrow. I'm telling you now. We need to discuss it. I can't allow this to happen. If you don't agree with me, you're going to have to pull this child out of my arms with me screaming and yelling." As far as I was concerned, it was not going to happen. We had a deep, emotional discussion about it for two hours. Initially, he was very resistant. At midnight all of a sudden he changed his mind and was in complete agreement with me. I thought he was kidding when he said, "OK, we won't do it." I didn't want him doing it [agreeing] because I pushed him into a corner. That's what happened to me. I got pushed into a corner by my family. Everyone pressured me into doing it. He was for real. He really agreed that he didn't want to do it. He realized that this was against his own beliefs.

David explained,

Why should we harm the kid? You don't snip your daughter. I just felt that if she felt that strongly about it, it's not as if we're observant of every other Jewish law. Why should I be so adamant about one that's harming my child?

Dana continued,

We called the mohel the next morning and canceled. I'm so relieved. We told our family as they got here, and we just did our own ceremony. It felt real special to us. . . . I feel confident in what I did. I never had any second thoughts about it. Every time I change his diaper, I feel so good that we didn't do it.

Childhood Memories of Being at a Bris

Studies, personal accounts, and our own experience confirm that the ability of adults to deny experience is well developed. However, children cannot deny reality so easily because their defenses are weaker. I know of two adults who witnessed circumcisions when they were children; both were about eight years old at the time. I met Zipora Schulz following my presentation on circumcision at a Jewish conference. She related this story of her childhood experience at a ritual circumcision:

> I walked into the room by mistake. I saw it [the circumcision] happen. I remember the baby crying and crying for a long time. People seemed happy about it. It seemed horrible and insane to me.[31]

She insists that she will not circumcise if she has a son in the future. Jeffrey Felshman was also at a Jewish ritual circumcision.

> One detail remains in my mind almost 30 years later. Screaming. The screaming was like none I've heard from any baby before or since. My cousin's grandfather was a doctor . . . and he assured us kids that the baby didn't feel any pain. It also was the first time a doctor expressed an opinion to which I responded, silently, "Bullshit."[32]

That experience helped to give Felshman the courage to keep his own son intact.

This unusual incident is related by the mother of a young child who had been circumcised.

> My son Matthew is about two years older than his cousin. We were at his cousin's bris, and the mohel got there really late. Matthew was walking around talking and playing with the adults. When the mohel walked in, Matthew stopped dead in his tracks and let out this scream like God knows what just happened. He just looked at the mohel and screamed. He ran out of the room and hid. The mohel was really a nice guy, not a big, menacing-looking person. He blended right in with the crowd that was there. Others who were total strangers walked in and didn't get any kind of a reaction from Matthew. The mohel was the same one who circumcised Matthew. People were asking, "Do you think he remembers?"[33]

6

Conflicts and Questions

As we have seen in the preceding chapters, close examination of circumcision, its meaning, and its ramifications reveals the presence of deep ethical, intellectual, and emotional conflicts among both Jewish men and Jewish women. Yet the impact of the practice on the Jewish community continues to go unrecognized. Repression of these conflicts about circumcision undermines individual and community integrity.

Lisa Braver Moss related her experience:

> I had profound doubts about my decision [to circumcise]. But because open discussion of Brit Milah seems to be discouraged in the Jewish community, I experienced my doubts privately and without comfort. . . . Thus, a rite intended to inspire feelings of Jewish unity evoked in me a sense of loss and alienation.[1]

Denying one's own truth results in personal disempowerment. Miriam Pollack asks, "If a woman is made to distrust her most basic instinct to protect her newborn child, what feelings can she ever trust?"[2] Parents who feel forced into making a decision that conflicts with their better instincts may harbor feelings of resentment against the community and tradition to which they feel compelled to conform.

Circumcision conflicts not only with feelings and experience but also with some traditional Jewish values and laws. For example, according to Jewish law, the human body must not be cut or marked (Lev. 19:28). By removing a part of the penis, circumcision involves the cutting and marking of male genitals.

Reason, Knowledge, and Understanding

Rabbi Milton Steinberg explains that Judaism

> places understanding among its supreme purposes, and in the further
> sense that it believes in knowledge as a key to understanding. But
> neither knowledge nor understanding is attainable without inquiry,
> debate, and the right to make up one's own mind. By its nature,
> then, Judaism is averse to formal creeds which of necessity limit and
> restrain thought.[3]

Even if one accepts circumcision as a divine commandment, Jews,
as partners with God, reserve the right to question and argue with
God. Regarding the covenant, Rabbi Eugene Borowitz states that
"each partner participates in it in full integrity; neither one is
master, neither one is slave; both can make their demands, each
partner saying, if necessary, a painful but self-respecting 'No.' "[4]

Based on these values, many Jews freely choose not to practice
many other rituals and laws. Forgoing circumcision is more
difficult. It is not unusual for new parents to choose circumcision
for their son and not be able to offer any rational justification. It is
noteworthy that many Jews who otherwise tend to value reason
and experience highly find it necessary to suspend reason and
experience when making a decision about circumcision.

*Growing evidence of the harmful effects of circumcision and
the doubtfulness of medical arguments for the procedure compel
us to apply reason and experience to the decision.* Whether circumcision is performed by a mohel or a doctor, there are inherent
risks. Even without complications, the infant experiences extreme
pain in the most sensitive part of his body. Though more research
is needed, behavioral and psychological effects have been reported in the literature. Both ancient and contemporary reports
agree that circumcision diminishes future sexual sensation.

Members of the Jewish community are just as likely as anyone
else to misunderstand the effects of circumcision, possibly even
more so. Since circumcision is so routinely expected of Jewish
male infants, perhaps many parents do not want to educate themselves about it because they believe that becoming informed may

create even more conflict and emotional distress and make the decision more difficult. Those who do take the time to learn about circumcision are often surprised and even shocked by what they discover. If they begin to question circumcision, and gain knowledge and understanding of the practice, they then face the added responsibility of making an ethical choice.

Ethics and Human Rights Considerations

Judaism values ethics above both doctrine and reason. Rabbi Steinberg explains, "For all its heavy intellectualism it [Judaism] sets morality above logic, the pursuit of justice and mercy over the possession of the correct idea."[5] How do we begin to justify the practice of circumcision on moral or ethical grounds? It is significant relative to this question that, according to an authoritative book on Judaism, "the Torah prohibits the torture or causing of pain to any living creature."[6] Given what we know about the consequences of circumcision, our conscience and Jewish law (Lev. 19:11; Exod. 23:1; Jos. 24:14) obligate us to be open and honest about this information.

In addition, if given a choice, would we consent to being circumcised? (Because of adult resistance to the procedure, Reform Jews have not required circumcision of converts since 1892.[7]) If not, then considering Hillel's encapsulation of Judaism: "What is hateful to you, do not to your fellow-creature" (Sab. 31a), should we force circumcision on another?

Significantly, though their wisdom expressed on many other subjects has been timeless, virtually all that has been written by rabbis about circumcision over the centuries ignores the infant's experience. Jewish adults today tend to have the same attitude. An infant being circumcised is restrained (typically by straps in a hospital, by adult hands during the bris) while having part of his body cut off. Imagine yourself in the same situation. *From the infant's perspective*, this is a physical attack. His physical struggle to escape and his piercing screams are evidence of an appropriate response to attack. It is a violation of Torah commandments to physically assault or harm another person (Exod. 21:18–27). The humanity of the newborn infant and his awareness, perception, sensitivity, and meaningful responsiveness are generally over-looked by adults, though these capabilities have been thoroughly documented by the latest research.[8]

We should listen more attentively to the child's feelings about circumcision. Author and childbirth educator Rosemary Romberg did not circumcise her seven-year-old son.

> When I explained circumcision to him, his face took on a frightened expression as he cupped his hands over his genitals and loudly de-clared, "That is never going to happen to me!!"[9]

It is appropriate to ask, Whose foreskin is it? There can be only one answer—it's the infant's foreskin. Taking it from him by force would cause him a loss. Furthermore, Jews have a moral obligation to help those who are helpless. Newborn infants are helpless. They need us to protect them from pain and loss. "You shall not stand idly by the blood of your neighbor" (Lev. 19:16) also implies a duty to help. It appears that in some important ways circumcision does not express Jewish ethical values; it is in con-flict with them.

Jews value human rights but have not yet addressed the issue of Jewish male infants having a right to physical integrity, a right recognized by Amnesty International as applying to all individuals. Human rights documents such as the Universal Dec-laration of Human Rights and the United Nations Convention on the Rights of the Child affirm that children shall be protected from physical injury and traditional practices prejudicial to health. Thus, parents have the *power* to circumcise, but do they have the *right* to circumcise? Given whose foreskin is being cut off, who is the proper person to make that decision? Do parents have the right to do anything they want to their children? Does conforming to religious or cultural practice entitle us to violate another person's rights? (Jewish law recognizes a newborn infant as a person if the infant has been born after a full-term pregnancy.[10])

Those who would deny that an infant has a right to physical integrity must answer the question, Does anyone have this right?

And if so, at what age does one acquire this right? What happens to fundamental principles and support for them when we make exceptions?

Jewish Culture and Male-Female Relationships

Aviva Cantor, author of *Jewish Men, Jewish Women* asks, "Why are American Jewish women and men experiencing low self-esteem and difficulties in their relationships with each other?"[11] These difficulties are evident in the high rate of intermarriage and the animosity demonstrated by male attitudes and behavior toward Jewish women. Jewish men degrade their mothers and stereotype them as overprotective. The JAP stereotype of the Jewish woman is also degrading and is often supported by Jewish men. These misogynist male attitudes and verbal attacks hurt and demean Jewish women. In addition, spousal abuse is a serious problem in all parts of the Jewish community across the United States and in Israel.[12] This behavior suggests a widespread anger in Jewish men toward Jewish women that remains unexamined. Of course, Jewish male anger toward and distrust of women may arouse a similar response in women.

The discord between Jewish men and women is not new. Misogyny and distrust of women are common in early rabbinic Judaism. An example is "He who speaks too much with women invites evil."[13] The Talmud has many references to unhappy marriages and male dissatisfaction with women.[14] After studying circumcision and gender in the ancient rabbinic texts, Rabbi Lawrence Hoffman concludes that circumcision has an effect on Jewish culture.

> To speak bluntly, what I found in this study surprised me (though perhaps, in retrospect, it shouldn't have). What is more, it made me very uneasy. . . . What I was not prepared for was the centrality of this ritual for Jewish culture as a whole, the very clear way that the symbolism of circumcision marked off the binary opposition between men and women, an opposition that I now take to be very basic to early rabbinic Judaism. . . . I forgot that for centuries official Jewish culture was—and still largely is—in the hands of the very

men who fashioned the rules of circumcision. Their obsession with circumcision turns out to have broad implications for the way they spelled out Jewish culture as a whole.[15]

The rabbis who created the rules for circumcision believed that men are "controlled" but that women "pose a constant threat of disorder, impulsive behavior, a failure of self-control."[16] Because of their categorical distrust of women, these men made sure that men had the power to control society. Though the balance of power is shifting because of activism by women, the dominance of male power is still a serious issue to be resolved within Judaism.

How does male distrust of women relate to circumcision? Let's look at theory and clinical experience. Erik Erikson's theory of psychosocial development includes eight chronological stages. In the first stage, the core issue is basic trust in the caretaking environment.[17] This theory is supported by the clinical experience of various mental health practitioners including psychiatrist Rima Laibow, who uses leading-edge techniques and reports,

> Events which impact upon the child's ability to trust mother may have long-term consequences in all areas of growth and development. . . . When a child is subjected to intolerable, overwhelming pain, he conceptualizes mother as both participatory and responsible regardless of mother's intent. . . . The consequences for impaired bonding are significant. . . . Circumcision is an enormous obstacle to the development of basic trust between mother and child.[18]

This statement, based on more than twenty years of clinical observations of children and adults who have reexperienced events of early infancy,* calls on us to see the world through the eyes of the newborn infant. That world centers on the mother. As a result, even though the physician or mohel does the circumcising, and the father may have made the final decision to circumcise, the newborn infant connects the experience to the mother. Because the experience is repressed, the connection between the event and

---

* Though there is controversy connected with this type of clinical work, considerable evidence supports the validity of these experiences.

the mother is also repressed. The loss of trust and the disruption of bonding are connected.[19] Distrust is also associated with neurobiological changes.[20]

In general, when a person is perceived to be responsible for inflicting pain and loss on another, the relationship is adversely affected by the resulting distrust and emotional distance. Inevitably, the distrust of one person develops into mutual distrust and separation. It would seem that the deeper the pain and loss, the deeper the distrust. It is possible that the extreme pain and loss of circumcision may engender deep distrust.

Infants themselves have exhibited behavior after circumcision that suggests distrust. The following personal account relates to the infant's ability to respond appropriately to the circumcision experience. Mary Conant, an obstetrical nurse, has observed circumcised infants who cover their genitals with their hands when their diapers are changed. Intact infants do not do this. One can plausibly infer from this behavior that circumcised infants may fear further damage to their genitals and may not trust their caretaker.

Trust is a prerequisite for intimacy. If circumcision and its traumatic effects disrupt the development of basic trust in infancy, the potential for intimacy in later life may be impaired. The possible connection between circumcision and difficulty with intimacy is consistent with theory, research, and clinical experience associated with trauma. Emotional withdrawal and avoidance of feelings related to intimacy is a common long-term effect of trauma.

According to the psychological literature, the effects of the circumcision experience on the child's feelings toward the mother may be more than withdrawal and distrust. A thirteen-year-old boy in psychoanalysis was profoundly affected by his circumcision at two years, eight months and regarded his mother as a malicious attacker.[21] Similarly, in a study of twelve Turkish boys who were circumcised between the ages of four and seven, the children perceived their mothers as the mutilators and directed aggression at them.[22] More reports and studies would be helpful, but they are not yet available.

How much does infant circumcision contribute to male distrust of women? We do not know, but viewing all women as "pos[ing] a constant threat of disorder, impulsive behavior, a failure of self-control" suggests an early trauma. It may be that, *from the infant's perspective* while he is having his penis cut, he is experiencing betrayal by his mother at a very vulnerable time in his life. As we learn more about circumcision and its effects, we realize that, like other traumas, it is possible that circumcision can have a long-term effect on beliefs, attitudes, and behaviors.*

---

* For a discussion of infant memory, recovered memories of circumcision by children and adults, and potential effects of circumcision trauma on adults, see *Circumcision: The Hidden Trauma.*

7

Preventing More Pain

Breaking the Silence

The primary way that circumcision is perpetuated in the Jewish community is through silence. The silence surrounding circumcision is a certain indication that there is something to hide. (As I have said earlier, the lack of response typically accompanies a lack of awareness.) If the parental experiences and responses reported in these pages are any indication, many Jews could be harboring very painful feelings about circumcision. The suppression of these feelings lends support to the practice. Continuing to circumcise is easier than confronting the pain.

Fear is another emotion motivating the decision to circumcise. Fear is often based on illusion. For example, those who have been afraid to question or even talk about circumcision have the illusion that they are alone with their thoughts, although many share the same concerns and are also afraid to express themselves. The fear and silence are contagious. This silence and the fact that circumcision is common practice help to create an illusion of agreement and support for circumcision.

The decision to circumcise is also fueled by a fear of rejection. Some parents fear their son will not be accepted if they choose not to circumcise. There is no evidence to support this fear. To the contrary, reports from American Jewish intact males indicate that their circumcision status has not been an issue for them, their friends, or their parents.[1] There are rabbis who would accept an intact boy as a Jew and lead a bar mitzvah ceremony for him.

Among them is Rabbi Schachter-Shalomi who says, "Circumcision is only one of the 613 commandments, and I would encourage him to fulfill the others."[2] Would you reject someone solely because he was not circumcised? This would not be consistent with deeply cherished Jewish values, including the precept to love your neighbor as yourself (Lev. 19:34).

One reason that circumcision is not challenged is the prevailing belief that the practice will never change and that it is useless to try to change it. People are most likely to conform (in this case, circumcise) when they believe there is no dissent. The silence on the issue supports this belief. The continued widespread compliance of yielding to the pressure to circumcise and then remaining silent fuels these beliefs about the practice, encourages the continuance, and so forth.

Evidence of suppressed feelings and examples of breaking the silence surrounding circumcision are growing. Rabbi Hoffman tells of a discussion about circumcision with fifteen young male and female rabbis. Each spoke personally.

> As we went around the room, several of these young rabbis related the case of their own son's circumcision, about which, it turned out, they frequently harbored intense rage—rage at themselves for allowing it to happen, and in some cases rage at the mohel who had done it and botched the job. Only here, in the intimacy of a class composed in large part of close friends, did they feel comfortable telling their tales. Stories proved cathartic; at one point people cried.[3]

At a Jewish women's conference, members of a discussion group talked about circumcision. "Judy speaks first: 'I'm so glad to be here because I've never even talked about this before—I thought I was the only one who worried about it.' So did we all. One by one, the stories pour out."[4]

As these examples demonstrate, open discussion will reveal to us that there is much that has been assumed, there is much we do not know, and there is much we feel that has not been expressed. Disclosure of these personal feelings can facilitate a deeper connection with others. Because there is so much hidden discomfort and deep feeling about circumcision, if only a relatively few people speak out against this practice, we can have an effect on a surprising number of others. Hearing a few speak out will make it safer for others to speak out too. Like silence, speaking out is also contagious. Attitudes toward circumcision will change when we are willing to risk speaking out about it.

A major victory in breaking the silence occurred on September 21, 1995, when the BBC showed *It's a Boy* to 2.1 million British viewers.[5] This critical documentary on circumcision was produced and directed by Victor Schonfeld, a father who regrets having his son circumcised. Calls by Jews to the station after the program numbered over two thousand and were overwhelmingly supportive of Schonfeld's message. Subsequent feature stories, opinion columns, and news reports were generally favorable as well.

Jenny Goodman, a psychotherapist and participant in the documentary, summarizes,

> Overall, people have been saying, "Oh, thank God somebody is saying this. Yes, we've got to stop doing it." It's been quite extraordinary. I've been getting phone calls from all sorts of people, whom I thought would be really angry, saying, "Good for you. We've got to talk about it, and we've got to change it." It's unbelievable, actually. It's had such a powerful effect. All the Orthodox are upset, but they haven't been able to say anything coherent. They've just got no defense. They haven't been able to find a decent argument in favor of it. What has become really apparent is that the battle has been to get the debate to happen, and that once the debate happens, the defenders have no defense.[6]

The documentary brought to the surface feelings about circumcision that had been submerged. In a column written after the broadcast, Rabbi Jonathan Romain said,

> What stunned me most of all was the number of Jews I met—synagogue-going Jews from all denominations—who said that it echoed some of their *long-held* worries about the subject. "It gave a voice to everything I had felt for ages, but had been afraid to say," was a common reaction. I have lost count of expectant mothers who told me: "I'm praying for a girl."[7]

Circumcision in Perspective

We are a people who ask questions. The question of circumcision is one of the most difficult and challenging we have ever faced. There will be those who claim that questioning circumcision weakens Judaism, but I would argue that they underestimate the power and ignore the purpose of Judaism. Furthermore, we know from personal experience that *avoiding difficult questions weakens people*. Honest questioning can only strengthen Judaism. Judaism has evolved through many changes already, some of which would shock the sages. It would also grow if we considered making changes in the way we welcome newborn male infants into the community (see Appendix G).

For some, the anxiety associated with questioning circumcision may be tied up with a concern that Jews might go on to question more aspects and practices of Judaism. But this, again, would be a positive development because deeper reflection strengthens Judaism. We must differentiate the many aspects of Judaism that serve us from the few that do not. Let's not "throw out the baby with the circumcision"!

And what would God say about questioning circumcision? One's inner voice does not necessarily conflict with the voice of God. As Rabbi Lawrence Kushner states, "The voice, if it be truly the voice of the Holy One of Being, speaks from both without and within. And it is the same voice."[8] If human beings are created in God's image and God is spiritual, then we and God have a common spiritual essence. We cannot trust the nature of God and mistrust ourselves. When we act on our deepest, purest impulses, God is acting through us.

Why is circumcision such a tenacious practice? I have mentioned fear, silence, and the power of conformity and beliefs. Another reason for the continuation of circumcision may be that it produces trauma, which results in behavior driven by extremely powerful psychological forces. A common long-term behavioral symptom of trauma is a compulsion to repeat the trauma. Circumcision is perpetuated mainly by men, with women often acquiescing in order to avoid conflict. (As we have seen, the conflict does not disappear but becomes internal rather than external.) For fathers, circumcising their sons could be a way of repeating the trauma of their own circumcision. (For further discussion, see *Circumcision: The Hidden Trauma*.)

As human beings, we tend to act out our repressed feelings on those who are weaker. We defend hurting others by creating rationalizations. For example, though circumcision is a subtraction, ancient rabbinic documents explain that a male is not "complete" until he is circumcised.[9] We also deny the infant's humanity by believing that the infant does not feel or remember pain. Such flawed thinking (as with current health claims, see Chapter 2) gives us "reasons" to pass the practice on to our children. By necessity, these "reasons" for circumcision sometimes employ conflicting logic, even irony.

Another long-term post-traumatic symptom is a desire to reclaim what was lost during the trauma. Personal accounts, clinical experience, and research reports tell us that circumcision disrupts the bond between mother and child. In my view, the covenant with God that has been used to justify Jewish circumcision may be a displaced effort to reclaim the true "covenant" that is our birthright—the bond between mother and child. It is also no coincidence that explanations for circumcision include a desire for God's protection. This is an idea generated by men who received no protection when they were circumcised as infants. Could the ancient attempt to "appease" God also be connected with repressed fear related to circumcision?

For the infant, circumcision is a sacrifice. The possibility of a father not requiring this sacrifice from his son may bring to the surface some of a father's feelings about his own circumcision. If fathers were to relent and not circumcise their sons, it would be as if Jewish men had to pay a high mandatory initiation fee to join an organization and then changed the rules to allow new members to join for free. So for many men the circumcision decision becomes a choice between allowing their sons to keep something that was taken from them, or acting out their pain by inflicting the loss on their sons. Given a father's compulsion to circumcise his son, a mother who opposes the practice must have strong conviction and act on her instincts to protect the child. (Of course, there are also situations in which the father opposes circumcision and the mother insists on it.)

It is not only the circumcised baby boy who has sacrificed something. We all have sacrificed—our integrity, our truth, and our connections. The practice of circumcision is not the first example of a cultural group demanding that its members sacrifice their truth to preserve an illusion. There are examples of similarly motivated practices throughout history. And Jews are not the only people who pass trauma on to their children in the form of a cultural practice. Non-Jewish Americans and other cultures also participate in such practices. The lessons of circumcision remind us that we must never set aside our feelings, instincts, and questions out of fear. We need each other to respond honestly and openly to what we experience.

We also need to remind ourselves of the difference between *what* we are doing and *why* we are doing it. If I forcefully cut off one of your healthy fingers, my reason would make no difference to you, even if I sincerely believed that amputating your finger was for your own good. Your experience of the event would be the same—pain, shock, horror. In the case of circumcision, what we are doing to the infant is cutting off a part of his penis. No explanations can change that fact. Our reasons, whether they involve religious belief, cultural conformity, or pleasing a relative, may make *us* feel better, but they *make no difference to the infant.*

Exploring Thoughts and Feelings

Traditions and rituals can provide a valuable function. But not all of them serve us equally well. There are timeless truths, and there are time-bound cultural beliefs and practices. A growing number of Jews conclude that circumcision is one of the latter.[10]

Circumcision is not the universal constant in Jewish life that it is assumed to be. Circumcision has not always been practiced by Jews. Even the form of the procedure has changed since ancient times. Many Jews tend to circumcise because of the belief that "it's something you have to do as a Jew." A few even take the position that circumcision "is not subject to debate,"[11] yet blind conformance is antithetical to Jewish values. Such a serious act as cutting off a normal, healthy, functioning body part demands a compelling justification.

The more we learn, think, and feel about circumcision, the more we see that it is not a topic we can dismiss lightly. Parents are advised to explore their thoughts and feelings with care. Because they are themselves circumcised, men in particular are encouraged to examine and share their feelings. By the time parents hear their son's painful cries, notice the feeling in their guts, and ask, "Why are we doing this?" it is too late.

It may be helpful to think about the following points and ask yourself some questions:

1. Your child's welfare is the primary consideration.
2. Circumcision, like any other surgical procedure, has risks. It is also irrevocable; an intact male still has options. If in doubt, the conservative choice is not to circumcise.
3. Would you circumcise your son if most Jews did not?
4. The fact that a father is not aware of any negative effects from circumcision does not necessarily mean there are none or that there will be none for his son.[12]
5. If you can't think of a convincing reason to circumcise your son, be aware that you may create one to fill the void.
6. If you are seeking to justify circumcising your son, carefully explore the presence of any underlying motivating factors. Beware of the development of a power struggle over this issue between you and your spouse or other family members. Then review item number 1.
7. Consider how you might answer your son when he is older and asks: "Why did you let someone cut off part of my penis?"
8. Imagine your son is circumcised. How do you feel?
9. Imagine your son is not circumcised. How do you feel?
10. Talk to others, but do not let yourself be pressured into doing something contrary to your own feelings.

A father who regrets his son's circumcision has another suggestion: "I urge you to attend a circumcision if you are considering one for your son. Feel what he feels. How would you feel being tied down and cut?"[13] When you attend, stand up close so that you can see the infant and the procedure. If you feel averse to doing this, what does your reaction tell you?

Next Steps

Parents' doubts and uneasiness about circumcision are real and justified. Routine hospital circumcisions are being convincingly challenged. Some doctors and nurses (including a few Jewish ones) refuse to participate in circumcisions.[14] As new information and arguments become more widely known, even more Jews may begin to question circumcision, and the pressure to reconsider circumcision within the Jewish community could increase.

It is not only in the United States that circumcision is being questioned. In countries where circumcision is not common, the procedure is receiving increasing scrutiny. The British authority on medical ethics, the General Medical Council, is considering taking an ethical stand that would effectively prohibit British doctors from doing circumcisions.[15] The Law Commission of the United Kingdom is also investigating the practice. In Australia the Queensland Law Reform Commission has requested that the Jewish community submit information to justify the ritual.[16] As circumcised men in these countries recognize and express the harm they have experienced from circumcision, authorities are compelled to respond.

International events should provide additional incentive for Jews to take action and confront the issue ourselves. We need time to go through this process. All interests would be best served if we simply faced circumcision honestly and openly, sooner rather than later. Opportunities to meet, learn, and express thoughts and feelings about circumcision in a safe and supportive environment would be helpful. Respectful and compassionate talking and listening would assist healing. The wisdom, feelings, and experiences of women are particularly important to this process.

At the ceremony without circumcision for his newborn son, Moshe Rothenberg expressed similar ideas to his friends and family:

> We are a wonderfully diverse people, and sometimes we forget that difference is a good thing. Each of us brings different thoughts, actions, and beliefs into what is collectively called Judaism. Today, the Jewish world is deeply involved in serious disputes . . . , and this ceremony, what is and what is not being done today, creates apparently another. I appeal to each of us to wrestle with our own beliefs, inside ourselves and with each other, respectfully. I appeal that we learn to disagree, rather than think that what we are doing is always right. Only then, to me, will our true sense of community thrive.[17]

Those in leadership positions in the Jewish community have a special obligation to facilitate discussion of this issue. This is more likely to happen with our encouragement and support. The bottom line is that the responsibility for questioning circumcision rests with all of us.

Potential Benefits of Forgoing Circumcision

If circumcision is not performed, the immediate beneficiary is the infant. He will be spared the overwhelming pain. And he will have a natural intact penis capable of natural sexual response.[18] Potential psychological problems will be avoided.[19]

Parents who decide not to circumcise their son will gain the freedom, power, and self-respect that comes to those who act in conformance with their own convictions. Love motivates us to protect others from pain and harm. Peace of mind comes from making this decision out of love, rather than out of fear and anxiety. In addition, the exploration and expression of feelings related to the decision can bring a couple closer together.

Support can come from where it is least expected. Natalie Bivas was surprised that both her own and her husband's families accepted their decision not to circumcise their son without any argument, but she was reluctant to share her decision with her temple women's group for several years. When she finally talked about it, she was amazed at the sympathy she received. A lot of women in the group said that they had circumcised their sons but that they didn't feel good about it.[20]

A central purpose of Judaism is *tikkun olam*, the repair and healing of the world. Much of the pain in the world is the result of repeating old harmful patterns of behaviors. By breaking a chain of pain, forgoing circumcision contributes to our healing. As we heal from this pain, we will be better able to heal others and reach our ethical and spiritual potential.

Many of the ideas and approaches used to question circumcision are associated with traditional Jewish values. This demonstrates that they are worthy values to guide us. We can marvel at the wisdom of the ancient sages. Sharing these values can give us the connection to the past that we seek. This connection is especially meaningful because it can be genuinely felt and freely experienced, rather than forced by conformity.

As more Jews feel safer to openly question the value of circumcision, the pressure to circumcise will wane. For those who want a ritual, a more joyous, personally meaningful one can be created. As stated in a letter to the editor of a Jewish magazine, Judaism will remain

> rich, multifaceted and spiritually and personally satisfying . . . long after we find a way of welcoming Jewish males into the world as an affirming covenant of life and not as a bond of pain.[21]

The practice of circumcision is rooted in our culture, but as more of us are recognizing, it is far from automatic; it is a choice.

New information, reasoned inquiry, gut feelings, personal experience, and Jewish ethical values together make a strong case for keeping a male infant the way he is born—natural and whole.

Appendix A

My Experience with Circumcision

Nancy Wainer Cohen

Ms. Cohen is the author of three books on cesarean birth and related issues. She has a circumcised twenty-two-year-old son. This statement is based on an interview in 1994.

Whenever I talk about that time [my son's circumcision] I also mention that I had a cesarean section. I was so debilitated myself, it was several weeks before I was able to care for him. I felt guilty, tired, overwhelmed, depressed, and angry. I had all these enormous feelings initially, and I didn't know what to do with them. I did express them and was met mostly with "You're nuts. You have a healthy baby. What are you complaining about? Some women can't have babies." But that didn't help me. I needed somebody to affirm what was going on for me. I think my husband got frightened and worried. . . .

I knew the day my son was circumcised that it wasn't the right thing to do, and I didn't have the energy, given where I was at, to fight real hard. My husband is from a very traditional Jewish background. [For him] there was no choice. You just did this. We had a mohel who came to the hospital. I didn't sleep the whole night before because I didn't want them to cut my son. I felt helpless and sort of backed into a corner. I said I wished he didn't have to be cut, but I was drugged and could barely get out of bed myself. Very reluctantly, I allowed it. I didn't want a celebration at my house. I didn't want a traditional bris where everybody drinks and celebrates. This was no cause for celebration. . . .

I heard him cry during the time they were circumcising him. The thing that is most disturbing to me is that I can still hear his cry. . . . It was an assault on him, and on some level it was an assault on me. . . . I will go to my grave hearing that horrible wail, and feeling somewhat responsible, feeling that it was my lack of evolvement. It was my lack of awareness, my lack of consciousness. I did the best I could, and it wasn't good enough. Always in the back of my mind I've thought, "I wish he hadn't been cut." I have apologized to him numerous times.

I don't know what he would have been like had he not been circumcised. But I really believe there was a personality change that day—from a calm and sweet little baby to a very quiet and sort of withdrawn child. Something was strange. [Now] he says he's OK. He's loving, and yet he's distant. I really do believe that it had something to do with the circumcision. . . .

I've done a lot of reading about the fact that we're mammals, and that we really have not owned our mammalian nature. As a mammal, if I had not been brainwashed by the medical community and subjected to the cultural pressure, I would have taken my baby into my arms, and I would have fought to the death before I would have allowed them to take him away from me to get circumcised. I'm getting in touch with a new part of me. I don't know what to do now except just think about it and constantly just love my son the best I can. I just want to let him know that he is incredibly precious to me and that there won't come a time again when I won't protect him. I may make some mistakes, but I think they will be coming from a slightly different place.

My daughter was born in 1979, and I was praying that she wouldn't be a boy. That's when my husband and I started to have discussions. One of them led to a pretty intense argument which was really scary for me. We rarely argued. We always had a nice rapport. We mostly agreed on things in the early years of our marriage. This argument was devastating because I said to him if it was a boy, if I had to take my child and run to Canada, I wasn't going to allow him to be cut. We had not resolved that issue.*

---

* It is not unusual for some people to take a nonnegotiable position for or against circumcision. In certain relationships, a conflict over circumcision can lead to serious consequences. Ideally, it would be advisable for couples to discuss the topic before a pregnancy, or even before marriage when sharing views about children.

After the birth he said, "We had a little girl. We're not having any more children. We don't have to deal with this." I eventually said to him, "We *do* have to deal with this because we're going to have grandchildren and because I am not sure that I want to live with somebody who doesn't share my basic beliefs, really strong basic beliefs about violence and abuse and parenting and all kinds of things." So it did become an issue in our marriage even though we didn't plan to have any more children. He kept saying, "What is the matter with you? You're crazy. We don't need to deal with this." I said, "We *do* need to deal with it."

It wasn't until I wrote the chapter called "Sheer Madness" in *Birthquake* this past year and asked him to sit down and read what I had written about circumcision that he finally looked at me and said, "We made a mistake." At that point, I thought, "There's hope for us." He said, "It's obviously our children's decision to make, but I'm on your side. I will do what I can to help you to inform them so that they will make the right decision."

Everybody says that doing clitoridectomies is barbaric. Mutilating little girls is just horrific. Why have we not yet made that crossover to the fact that it's equally as horrific to mutilate little boys? It just doesn't make any sense on any level. There's no justification.

Appendix B

One Woman's Learning Process

*(This statement was prepared by a mother
who wants to remain anonymous.)*

This is the story of how I went from being pro-circumcision and never questioning it to becoming vehemently opposed to circumcision. The process of finding the inner courage to go against what was expected of me took about five years. It would have happened much sooner if I had had the information I wanted and talked with other like-minded people sooner. I feel forever blessed to have found the information and support before the birth of my son. Now I have no regrets, only appreciation for those who helped to illuminate my path.

I am a Jewish woman married to a Jewish man. I am proud of my Jewish heritage and often feel comforted by the spiritual aspects of my religion. I teach my ten-year-old daughter and six-year-old son Jewish songs and maintain our culture and holidays.

I grew up in a 99 percent Jewish community. What I now find confusing and intriguing is that many people questioned whether or not to observe the Sabbath or to keep kosher, but one topic was never discussed—circumcision (unless there was a bris, and then the discussion was where and when it would be held).

I first heard about people opting not to circumcise through my work with childbirth education. I was promoting my work at an exposition, and while I was taking a break, someone left a brochure written by Edward Wallerstein, a Jewish man, at my booth. It detailed many reasons not to circumcise. Though I was curious and open to learning new things, as a Jewish woman, I was not ready to challenge my traditions. I felt enraged.

In the few years that followed, I came into contact with midwives, lactation consultants, childbirth educators, and social workers who did not find circumcision necessary and/or opposed it, as well as parents who had opted not to circumcise. I felt I had to learn more, so I read various articles and a book called *Circumcision: An American Health Fallacy* by Edward Wallerstein [currently out of print].

Among other things, I learned about the lack of health benefits, the pain to the infant, and the risks of circumcision. I heard about negative psychological and sexual effects. My thoughts about circumcision began shifting. God or nature has created us perfectly, and each part has a function. After all, I still feel violated about my tonsillectomy at age five. Now that I understood that there were no medical reasons for circumcision and that there was a risk of complications, I wondered why American doctors still continue to perform the procedure.

Of all the conversations I had about circumcision, this one was pivotal. A colleague whom I admired informed me that she had attended a meeting at the United Nations to protest female circumcision worldwide. I did not know until that moment that female circumcision existed. I did not have to read or think. My reaction was in my gut. All at once I cringed. I was revolted and enraged, and in that split second I knew that I could never again support male circumcision. At that moment I understood the trauma that circumcision inflicts.

Despite my increased understanding, the religious reason was still tugging at me, and my husband opposed my views. How would I ensure that a future son of mine would be left intact? I felt the need to talk to other Jewish parents and uncircumcised Jewish men. I wanted support and information to find the courage and inner strength I needed to challenge both my family and a religious tradition that had persisted for thousands of years. Unfortunately, I did not have the support and information I needed by the time my first child was born. However, luckily for me and my child, my firstborn was a girl.

Finally, in the summer of 1987, I found the information and support I needed. I saw an article in *Mothering* magazine about an alternative ceremony for welcoming a newborn child into the Jewish community. I also found and talked with other Jews who did not circumcise their sons. Questions and ideas that came up during these conversations helped strengthen my resolve, though my husband still supported circumcision.

What if you and your husband do not stay together?
What if he dies or changes his mind?
Do not do what you cannot undo.
First, do no harm.
Let the boys decide for themselves. It's their body.

These conversations stimulated more self-questioning. I asked myself if I had a son, how would I ever explain to him that I knowingly allowed pain to be inflicted on him just because my family and religion expected it of me. It seems this would have broken an unspoken, fundamental trust in our relationship. Also if my son was one of those who suffered complications from the surgery, how would I ever forgive myself, and how would I ever explain why I had allowed this? I realized no apology would ever satisfy me.

While I was going through this time of self-questioning, a friend invited me to her son's bris. I had been to his home birth. The grandmother, using guilt and fear of rejection, had pressured the parents to have the circumcision. I shared information about circumcision with my friend, and I didn't want to go to the bris. However, after thinking about it for a long time, I decided to go to support my friend. Right before the circumcision, the father was crying. I wanted to say, "You don't have to go ahead with this. If you're crying, it shows something is not right."

I remember leaving the room when the circumcision was performed. My stomach was churning. My heart felt intense pain. My desire was to scoop the baby up and run away. I also wanted to scream, "Stop! This is unfair! I won't allow this! How can all of you stand around here and allow this? How can you pretend not to care or to be disturbed? How can you then go and eat and pretend all is well?"

I did not have the courage to speak at the bris. I was disappointed in myself and infuriated by this tradition that I felt we were forced to follow. I learned one thing from that bris. I would never for anyone, for any reason, attend another one. I cannot again betray myself and how I feel, and I could not in my heart support anyone who has decided to circumcise.

My reading, conversations, and experiences brought me into contact with Jewish people who had dared to live by their convictions despite the disapproval of others. At this point, despite my intensely strong desire to be accepted and approved by my religion and my family, I knew that I could not permit or perpetuate a custom that would inflict physical pain, emotional trauma, and possible medical complications on my child. I realized that if I ever had a son, my allegiance to my son and myself were the most important factors to consider.

When I discussed the issue of circumcision with my husband, he could not understand my viewpoint. This was not surprising, since I realized how long it had taken me to change my mind. However, he was not willing to learn about and explore the issue further. I was in pain, torn about what I felt in my heart about circumcision and how these feelings affected my husband. Even though my husband was not ready to reconsider his views, I had the inner strength, conviction, and support to insist on my position. Our second child was a boy, and he was not circumcised.

My mother-in-law withdrew for a while, but now we are close again. Other family members have accepted my decision. I have talked to both of my children, and they understand and agree with my decision to keep my son intact.

While writing this I realize that I was taught to be a good, quiet, little girl. I also was dependent on my family. I was afraid to disagree with my family because they would then withdraw and reject me. Now I understand the power my childhood fear has had over me. I am no longer afraid. Now when a person rejects me or withdraws from our relationship, I realize it is their immature response to my disagreement with them, and I no longer doubt my own thinking or my own goodness based on their response. While I have chosen to always leave the door open for forgiveness in my relationships, I no longer wait for this to happen. I surround myself with colleagues and friends who appreciate my goodness, admire my courage, and respect me for my openness and willingness to challenge both myself and the status quo for the good of all.

Now I have a strong sense of myself, and though I cherish my family ties, I would never again doubt or betray my values for someone else. Questioning circumcision has been a growth and maturation process for me. I am very grateful to the people who helped me to understand. I recommend getting informed and being strong and true to yourself. Years later, I look at myself in the mirror, and I am proud. I love myself. I did what I felt and learned was right.

I have decided that whenever I get invited to another bris, I will send information that helped me to make my decision. When I talk to some people they tell me, "It's too late. My son is already circumcised, and so this issue doesn't concern me anymore." I reply, "It's never too late to say you are sorry and that you regret your decision. It's not too late to get informed and spare your grandchildren and the children of your friends and neighbors. And it's not too late to heal your own guilt, regret, or pain."

Let's reach out to inform others, so that in decades to come we will have contributed to eliminating the pain to our precious newborns.

Appendix C

"The Circumcision Debate"

TIKKUN CONFERENCE ON JEWISH RENEWAL
New York City, November 6, 1994

(This discussion followed three presentations on circumcision: two supported the practice, and one, by Ronald Goldman, questioned the practice.)

FEMALE 1: (A previous comment was made attempting to justify circumcision by noting that birth is also painful.) The most serious problems occur when babies are circumcised on the second day before their blood clotting has set up. The eighth day is a very good time to circumcise babies. Babies who are circumcised in the hospital are tied down. Babies who are ritually circumcised have their legs held. They are held by somebody who loves them. They are not on a plastic board. The American Academy of Pediatrics did move toward saying circumcision was not a good thing. In 1989 they came out with a new position statement. And this is not for Jewish children. This is for children across the board. Families should make their decision based on the fact that there are some [potential] medical benefits from circumcision and there are some negative factors involved. People need to know both sides. Circumcision does reduce the risk of urinary tract infection in children. Circumcision does reduce the risk of penile cancer. It reduces the risk that a child or an adult will later have to have a circumcision for medical reasons which is much more painful. There is absolutely no evidence that psychologically we have damaged Jewish men.

The American Academy of Pediatrics has a strong position on this [circumcision]. It is not a negative thing. Parents can make their decision based on their needs. If somebody really doesn't want to do it, that's fine. I'm not saying that they should do it. I was able to stand there, and I went through the circumcision of my son and my two grandsons. For a few moments I was a little nervous. In addition, the use of wine, or a little grape juice or sugar water new studies have shown, anesthetize. The new study was just in the American Academy of Pediatrics journal. It does reduce the pain tremendously. In fact, they're talking about using that in other kinds of surgery in infants, in newborns, not just in circumcision.

RONALD GOLDMAN: I think a few other people want to comment. Let me just have about a minute. Not everything you said is accurate. I have documentation on everything I've said if people want to see that later. There is no controversy about the pain. There is no controversy about the severity of the pain. I don't want to get into the details of the studies, but as far as the American Academy of Pediatrics is concerned, they have not come up with one proven benefit. And this isn't the reason that Jews would circumcise. Health considerations are totally beside the point.

MALE 1: I would like to respond to everything that's been said [deep breath]. I really appreciate the opportunity to have this discussion here. And I want to talk about my personal experience with whether or not circumcision promotes Jewish connection and Jewish values [deep breath]. For the first twenty-two years of my life I felt absolutely no positive connection to Judaism. It disinterested me [with faster pace, anger building]. When I was in a Jewish place I wanted to run away. They weren't going to get one of those slippery little kipot (skullcaps traditionally worn by Jewish males) on my head. Men with tallit (fringed shawl worn during prayer) drove me up the wall. And that God-awful Maneschevitz wine—was disgusting. I always felt terrible when I had to drink it at Kiddush (a Sabbath blessing recited over wine).

I was a very spiritual person. I got involved in all kinds of new age spirituality and spiritual searching as well as the process of self-searching [deep breath]. One day I went into a support group for people working on recovering from the effects of early memories associated with sex. And suddenly I got terrified because there were all these people standing around there doing nothing. And I said this reminds me of some other time. And all the memories of my own circumcision came back to me, including, get this [emphatically]—slippery little kipot, tallit, and wine! And it all returned by association. And I uncovered this incredibly deep level of fear on top of my resistance to Judaism. And it was only after that, that I was able to open up to the positive and spiritual aspects of Judaism and begin my spiritual path that nine or ten years later has put me in the middle of rabbinical school [deep breath].

So speaking from personal experience, I do not have one bit of evidence that circumcision promotes positive Jewish continuity. And I'm also in the middle of this incredible conflict about it because I serve as the rabbi of a traditional Conservative congregation that would absolutely go ballistic if I said such things there. To make matters worse, we're expecting a baby in nine weeks. We have not decided to use ultrasound to determine the gender of the baby, but I have to find an elegant way of doing this.

I also want to say that I have developed an alternative circumcision ceremony that someone asked me to do once. And a lot of talk has been about creating meaningful life cycle events. The ceremony I created is similar to the traditional circumcision ceremony except that instead of cutting the little boy's penis, we cut a piece of cloth that the little boy was lying on. Everyone including the parents and [joyously] the grandparents who were originally against this thing, thanked me very much for coming to perform this ceremony. They said it was a beautiful ceremony. So I think that, yes, we can create meaningful connection without circumcision.

I also wonder why it is that so many Jewish men have a hard time connecting to Judaism. Why is it that in our most dynamic and active Jewish renewal communities, the women come forth first? I wonder why. I wonder if it has something to do with this. I wonder if there are more men who have that same just plain blank, flat resistance—I don't want to know, and it doesn't mean anything to me—that I had for similar reasons. I have to ask that question.

FEMALE 2: Some of you may have seen this is a very emotional topic for me, and I want to thank you, Ron. I think that the way you express the ethical problem for Jews today is so important. My husband and I had a child born at home three and a half years ago, and when my mother-in-law said, "I don't hear any discussion about the bris," I said, "There isn't going to be one." That was a decision for me. We knew we were having a boy through ultrasound, and what we had was a naming ceremony at home using all the same elements of the traditional ceremony with the exception of the cutting. The twenty relatives who were at the ceremony said it was for them the most moving ceremony they had been to [speaker is close to tears]. My husband was able to speak about the meaning of having a child, the meaning of the names, the Hebrew and English names, that we chose for the child.

The day I went into labor I was at the 92nd street "Y" (Young Men's and Young Women's Hebrew Association) reading books on Judaism trying to look for a reason to circumcise my son. I do not keep kosher. I observe Judaism in a very deep, meaningful way for myself in my home and chavurah settings. And I felt that after having a home birth and having this gentle soul with me for these days, to circumcise would have been simply because of the pressure of the masses. And that would not have been a decision with integrity for myself. So I'm really very thankful. I think I would very much like a copy of your paper. I think that you're opening this up.

I was very disappointed to read *Moment* magazine's articles about it a few years ago. It's just like what you're saying. Let's not get too deep into this in the Jewish community because this is going to be damaging. This is what I saw in one of my readings: "This is the last thing that keeps the Jewish people together." To impose that on someone, a family, cultural Jews, to pressure them to circumcise a son, to say that will be their connection to Judaism, when they themselves do not follow rituals and commandments, wreaks of a hypocrisy which I find very upsetting. And I feel, as you said, that all people, men, women, girls, and boys, need to find their way to Judaism, to a Judaism that's meaningful. And I hope that we can continue more discussions like this.

FEMALE 3: The pain of childbirth is a necessary, sensory experience that children have to go through. It's painful for the mother, but the squeezing of tissue, the massaging of tissue—children need to feel that. To say then go circumcise the boy is a terrible analogy. Children need to be born, and there are reasons for them being born vaginally.

FEMALE 1: When they are born through cesarean section they are equally healthy, and they don't have any problems.

FEMALE 4: I would just like to comment on a personal level. I'm a grandmother, and my granddaughter is a delight. I recall before she was born that my son and daughter-in-law said that if it were a boy, they would not have the circumcision ritual, even though my son, both my sons, were circumcised in the hospital. I guess I'm a cultural Jew. I'm not a religious one, but it was part of the tradition of family and belonging as a Jew. But I can understand what my son was saying now. He felt he could be a Jew as he felt being a Jew, but not necessarily making his son, if there were a boy, go through this ritual which he questioned. And which I question now, too, as a Jewish woman and feminist. That is not the only way of identifying as a Jew.

My background is public health. I remember several years ago a few pediatricians that I had worked with and one who had been my family's pediatrician went to many seminars on this question of circumcision for every baby boy. There was a group that took the position that it was not essential or recommended for positive health practice, though others took the other position. So there was controversy on it.

I feel very comfortable with this discussion. I'm delighted that there is openness about questioning [circumcision] or participating [in Judaism] however you want, and that [circumcision] is not critical for being a Jew.

FEMALE 3: I'm recently studying child development. Daniel Stern wrote a book called *The First Relationship*. He calls it the dance between the mother and the child, and also sometimes the missteps when the mother or any caregiver doesn't dance with the child, and maybe doesn't respond to the child's needs. There is something that happens to the child psychologically. And relating to it [circumcision], in terms of the crying, when you don't respond well to the child, the child will go into a state of limpness. And it will not even bother resisting anymore because nobody cares. It goes into a state of giving up. It's been noted. It's been seen many times.

And what is the point of saying, you've already experienced the pain of childbirth. Why add to that? Just look at it objectively, just the cruelty of it [circumcision]. I don't have any children, and I never thought about this subject until the thought of possibly having one in the next couple of years. Just the thought of it, if I ever have a male child, I would be totally against it. Just in my body, I feel it's wrong. I feel it. It's wrong. The thought of doing that to your own child just because it's been tradition—why keep up with old assumptions? Why are we so insensitive to the child, other than the fact that it must be for our own purposes? It's certainly not for the child. It's pretty clear. Most of us would be against girls' circumcision, if we thought about it. Why is that so different?

MALE 2: We have an eight-year-old son who was not circumcised. The decision was pretty simple really once we cleared up rather quickly there was no medical reason to circumcise him. The only issue became that of community and the incredible pressure from friends and relatives and the community at large. This is what you do, and so on and so forth.

We sort of half hide the fact that we didn't circumcise him. We don't generally discuss it in polite company and don't share it with a lot of people. I also wonder for myself, one of my fears for Paul (pseudonym) is the reaction that he may get as he gets older and he wants to marry a Jewish woman, if he's not one of the 50 percent who decide not to marry a Jewish woman, and that becomes an issue. That's a real fear. That's what I'm afraid of from my perspective. What have I done to him? Have I put him in a situation that as an adult he's going to have to get himself circumcised? That would be a horrible nightmare. We're just hoping that the Jewish community will come around in the next ten years before that happens to him so it isn't an issue for him.

The small piece about circumcision that Michael Lerner has in his book was actually one of the most disappointing sections of the book for me. In the beginning he spends a great deal of time talking about the chain of pain. Now we have to break that chain of pain. He talks about Abraham and how Abraham decided not to murder his child, how God stopped him from doing that. He talks about how he thinks he's hearing God's voice when he goes up there to kill his child, but then the voice who tells him not to kill Isaac, that's the real God's voice. I don't understand then why it's not then obvious that we're talking about two voices of God here also. We're talking about circumcision. It's not God's voice that's telling him to mutilate his child. It's that voice of the past. It's the voice of the past. Maybe the voice of pain.

FEMALE 5: I'm grateful for the opportunity to speak. I'm Paul's mother. I am and have always been crystal clear that I would never inflict harm on him. I had no ambivalence at all, ever. I think that children have so much pain. We all have so much pain in our lives. It feels very crazy to me to volitionally create something out of nothing and inflict such extreme pain.

So we didn't do it, and the reaction of friends was so bizarre. It was almost as if everybody was in a trance, and I mean that. I'm not being facetious. It's as if when you talk about circumcision, people who are otherwise rational, humanistic, caring, gentle, wonderful parents, good friends, talked about his covenant with God and how he wouldn't be a Jew. He is a Jew.

FEMALE 3: People are using generalizations. We say Jewish men are all circumcised, but most of them were circumcised in a hospital.

It wasn't even a brit milah. It was done by an obstetrician. It was a surgical procedure. Are they any more entitled, if you need a certificate, to get bar mitzvahed. We're dealing with so many falsehoods and assumptions that it's just incredible.

Appendix D

A Response to Traditionalists

Religious practices of traditionalists are not always consistent with divine commandments as written in the Torah. Here are a few examples:

In the Torah, adultery (Lev. 20:10), fornication by women (Deut 22:21), homosexual acts (Lev. 20:13), blasphemy (Lev. 24:16), insulting one's parents (Exod. 21:17), and stubbornly disobeying one's parents (Deut. 21:18–21) are all punishable by death. Obviously, these laws are no longer enforced by traditionalists. Of course, laws permitting slavery (Exod. 21:1–11; Deut. 15:12–18; Lev. 25:39–46) and animal sacrifices (e.g., Lev. 4:3, 4:23, 4:32, 5:7, 5:15) were abandoned.

In addition, according to Torah law, only a man can divorce his spouse (Deut. 24:1). This law was changed by rabbis to allow a woman to seek a divorce. With the help of the rabbinical court, a man can be made to comply. The Torah law which restricted inheritance to sons (Deut. 21:15–17) was also changed to allow transfer of property to daughters.

It is clear that even among traditionalists, changes in cultural attitudes can result in changes in traditional religious laws and practices. In this way Judaism is a living religion and the Torah is a living document.

Appendix E

Circumcision and Anti-Semitism

Imagine yourself being an intact, non-Jewish boy. At some point in your childhood you learn what Jews do to boys. How do you feel?

We tend not to appreciate what it is like for those who do not circumcise to be associated with people who do circumcise. However, as we learn more about circumcision and sensitize ourselves to the pain and harm it causes, our concern with the practice grows. Could the historical discomfort, distrust, or dislike of Jews be at least partly due to conscious or unconscious feelings that others have had about circumcision?

People tend to distance themselves from those who are perceived as different. By making Jews different, circumcision can separate Jews from others (in societies that do not circumcise). Ancient Greek and Roman writings reveal that circumcision was a significant reason for negative feelings toward Jews.[1]

One psychoanalyst and researcher concludes that "for the non-Jew, circumcision is at the root of Jewish 'strangeness.' "[2] Clinical experience confirms that circumcision often evokes horror in anti-Semitic personalities.[3] In *Nuremberg Diary*, author G. M. Gilbert, the prison psychologist at the Nuremberg Trial, writes that number one Nazi Jew-baiter Julius Streicher was obsessed with anti-Semitism. Insight into his feelings was revealed in private conversations. Streicher repeatedly referred to circumcision when speaking about Jews.[4]

Some anti-Semites fear that circumcision has a negative effect on Jewish men. According to psychoanalyst and author Rudolph Loewenstein,

> The sexual factor is one of the most powerful unacknowledged mo-
> tivations underlying anti-Semitism. In anti-Semitic literature the Jew
> was represented as a sexual pervert who took pleasure in raping and
> debauching "Aryan" women. . . . These representations are often as-
> sociated with Jewish circumcision.[5]

Circumcision also may stir fears of being cut in those who have
intact genitals. Various authorities have speculated on these connections.[6] Psychologist Gordon Allport, in his classic work *The
Nature of Prejudice*, notes that to other people the Jewish practice
of circumcision

> probably caused much consternation. . . . How much unconscious
> fear and sexual conflict this rite has aroused in the minds of non-
> Jewish people throughout the centuries is impossible to say. The in-
> timacy of the "castration threat" may play a large, if unconscious,
> part in the abhorrence of things Jewish.[7]

With our history of being oppressed, we are more likely to focus
on what other people have done to us, rather than to acknowledge
what we have done to ourselves. By practicing circumcision and
dismissing its effects, we put noncircumcising people in the
position of either confronting us about circumcision or ignoring it.
Since confronting us is seen as virtually hopeless and likely to
arouse resentment, they generally ignore their feelings about circumcision and consequently deny a part of their reality and themselves.
Because they do not feel safe to express themselves directly to
Jews about circumcision, perhaps some express their feelings
indirectly through their attitudes and behaviors toward us. Research in this area could provide valuable information.

Upon further reflection, it becomes clear that the deep psychological issues connected with circumcision are not limited to just
those who practice it. Others are also affected. Consequently, we
may find that addressing the issue of circumcision may not only
help to heal long-standing relationship problems within the Jewish
community; it may also help to improve our relationships with
noncircumcising, non-Jewish people.

Appendix F

Precautions for Parents of Intact Boys

If you choose not to circumcise your son, there are additional steps to take to insure his well-being.

Many doctors are not aware of normal foreskin development because they were not taught about this in medical school. They may force the retraction of a young boy's foreskin before it is ready. (Sometimes retraction doesn't happen naturally until as late as adolescence.) Forcing the foreskin back can cause pain and injury. Talk to your doctor to be sure that your son's foreskin will be left alone.

Before your son has an opportunity to see other boys' penises, explain to him why some other penises may look different. Let him know that he has a natural, complete penis while some others may have had a part cut off. Tell him why you chose to keep his penis whole. With this knowledge, he will understand the difference and appreciate that he is intact.

Appendix G

Alternative Rituals

Some Jews who choose not to circumcise but still want a ritual, change the ritual to omit the circumcision. They may include other ceremonial elements that are sensitive to the infant and the community. For example, something other than the infant's body can be cut to symbolize the circumcision. An alternative ritual, sometimes referred to as a naming ceremony or "bris shalom," may or may not be led by a rabbi. It has all the joy of the traditional ritual without the pain of the circumcision.

Some Jews may question alternative rituals, but according to Rabbi Eugene Cohen, 80 percent of American Jewish circumcisions already do not meet ritual standards.[1] Because the surgical procedure alone does not fulfill the religious requirement, and since many sons of Jewish parents are circumcised in a hospital by physicians, there is often no religious component to the event, and, some would say, no covenant with God. One could argue that a hospital circumcision no more fulfills the divine requirement than no circumcision. Where ritual is concerned, it is the meaning of the act and not just the act itself that is important.

In addition, the religious ritual should be performed with the "appropriate mindset."[2] But, this cannot be forced. As discussed earlier, many Jews circumcise their sons with great emotional conflict, reluctance, and regret. The alternative ritual allows for congruence of intention, attitude, action, and feeling.

The use of an alternative ritual has another advantage; it can be used for both male and female infants. The growing interest in an equivalent ceremony for girls illustrates how culturally-bound practices must change to be compatible with evolving values. Reformist observant Jews accept that each generation needs to create contemporary forms of expressing its connection to its religious tradition. Judaism, as a patriarchal religion, has been influenced by the women's movement.

Rabbi Joel Roth attempts to defend the patriarchal practice of circumcision by stating that "by physiology women cannot be brought into the covenant of Abraham by circumcision."[3] However, circumcision ceremonies are performed on African females as well as males.[4] There are various types of female genital surgery. The procedure analogous to circumcision would be to remove the clitoral hood. Physiology is not an excuse for exclusively male ritual surgery.

Rather than perform some kind of genital surgery on females, an idea that is repugnant and rejected by virtually all Jews, a ceremony without surgery for both sexes is the egalitarian solution.

The sample alternative rituals that follow are included to suggest options. They may be used as written or changed as desired for either a boy child or a girl child. The addition of personal statements by parents, family, and friends can make an alternative ritual especially meaningful.

Bris Shalom
adapted by Norm Cohen

A group of invited family and friends assemble at the parents' home for the occasion.

The honored participants, in order of appearance:
- the Jewish leader (*Chazzan*) of this ceremony
- an honored guest (*Sandak*): often he is the grandfather or sometimes the father, a patron of the child
- the mother and father
- godfather (*Kvatter*): passes the baby from the godmother to the Sandak
- godmother (*Kvatterin*): carries the baby into the room
- the baby boy, on his eighth day of life

The participants standby in a separate room. Family and friends wait in the room for the participants to appear. An empty chair is provided as a symbol for the presence of the prophet, Elijah. A cup of wine is poured.

The leader enters the room by himself and begins with the following passage from Genesis 22:10–12:

Abraham stretched forth his hand and took a knife. And the angel of the Lord called to him out of heaven and said, "Abraham, Abraham!" And Abraham said, "Here am I." And the angel said, "Lay not your hand upon the lad nor do anything to him."

A procession of the other honored participants begins. The baby is brought in last.

All (rise): *Ba-ruch Ha-bah!* Blessed is the one who has come!

Leader: *Ba-ruch Ha-bah!* Blessed is the one who has come for the Covenant on the eighth day!

> Blessed is the Lord our God, Creator of the universe, who has sanctified us with Your commandments.

> We assemble now to welcome this newborn into Your Covenant and into the community of Israel.

Parents: Blessed is the Lord our God, Creator of the universe, who has granted us life and sustained us and permitted us to reach this season.

> Blessed is the Lord our God, Creator of the universe, who has commanded us to welcome our son into Your Covenant.

> This child, created in Your image, is whole, complete, and perfect.

> We give to him Your Covenant of Peace.

> Amen.

Sandak (points to the chair of Elijah): This is the chair of Elijah the prophet, who is remembered as the protector of children.

The baby is passed from the godmother, to the godfather, and then to the *Sandak*. The *Sandak* now sits with him on the chair of Elijah.

Sandak (from Leviticus 19:28):
> And the Lord said, "You shall not make any cuttings in your flesh for the dead, nor imprint any marks upon you."

All: Let this baby be happy in this world,
> In the goodness of this home,
> In the holiness of this place.

Parents: Blessed it is that we are made holy with commandments
and are charged to keep the Covenant.

Blessed it is that we are made holy with commandments
and are charged with welcoming our child into the Covenant
of Sarah and Abraham.

All: As he enters into the Covenant so may he enter
into Truth,
into Love,
and into Happiness.

Leader (holds up a cup of wine):
*Ba-ruch ah-ta Ah-do-nai, el-o-hey-nu mel-ach ha-o-lam,
bo-rey pri ha-ga-fen.*

All: Blessed is the Lord our God, Creator of the universe,
who makes the fruit of the vine. Amen.

The leader passes the wine to the godparents. The godparents take
a drink of the wine and share it with the parents.

Leader: Blessed is the way of the universe which makes children
holy and beloved as their birthright, which keeps the laws
of the world in our flesh, and seals our offspring with a
mark of holy promise.

Parents: We pray that our son grows up in a world free of violence
and with great joy and peace.

All: Blessed are all who are assembled here and who join in this
holy Covenant.

Sandak (holds up the baby):
Give thanks to our Lord, for He is good.
His kindness endures forever!
This little one, may he become great!
Go forth, you are perfect!

The *Sandak* passes the baby to the mother and father.

Godparents: May this child thrive with his mother and with his
        father. Let his name be known among us as (the child's full
        name) son of (the parents' full names).

All: As he enters into the Covenant, so may he enter,
        into Truth,
        into Love,
        and into Happiness.

Leader: May the Lord bless us and keep us. May He make His
        countenance shine upon us, and be gracious unto us. May
        the Lord turn His face unto us and give us Peace. Amen.

All: Mazel Tov!

Naming Ceremony

The Naming Ceremony is a birth ritual intended for use in the liberal Jewish community. It applies equally to girls and boys and serves a number of purposes. In the Naming Ceremony the child is publicly introduced into the Jewish community. The child is formally given the name Jew, which she/he shares in common with other members of the community, and which serves as a basic symbol in her/his religious life. Also in the Naming Ceremony, the child is given her/his proper name, which signifies the reality and fundamental importance of her/his individuality. Those present at the ceremony represent the liberal religious community's affirmation of the right of the child to individuality, and the freedom implicit in this right. Thus the Naming Ceremony bestows upon a child membership in the Jewish religious community while affirming her/his freedom in that community to realize her/his special qualities as a unique human being. It goes without saying that the Naming Ceremony aids parents and community alike in the opportunity to rejoice in the pleasure of new human life.

Parents or Reader: *B'ruchim habaim.* Blessed are all who have come here on this happy occasion.

Parents or Reader (light candles): There is a new light in our/your hearts and in our/your home. These candles celebrate the birth of our/your child. Out of the creative darkness she/he has come. These candles celebrate her/his emergence into light. Fortunate the woman who knows the pangs of birth, for she has held a star. Fortunate the man who fathers a child, for he has held eternity in his arms. These candles celebrate the fire of our love out of which this child was created.

Parents or Reader: The unending generations of life reveal the unity of an everchanging universe. Hidden in birth and death, the roaring winds, and the gentle voices of loved ones lies the harmony of existence. As we gather here in community, we make manifest the unity of the universe that gave us all birth. *Shema yisrael adonai elohenu adonai echad. Baruch shem kevod malchutoe le-olam va-ed.*

Parents: Tomorrow is a mystery, and the day after is unknown. In awe we face our daughter's/son's tomorrows, all that this child may come to be. This warm softness is dreaming innocence. With our love and care we seek to make her/his dreams real in the world.

(A cup is filled with wine.)

Parents or Reader: This cup is the vessel of our hopes. It is filled with the new wine of a life just begun. The sweetness of its taste is the joy this child has brought. So many of our hopes cannot be spoken. They must be left in the heart's deep, silent places. *Baruch attah adonai elohenu melech haolam borai pre hagafen.*

Parents or Reader: On this _____ day of the month of _____ 19__, corresponding to the _____ day of _____, 57__, of the Hebrew calendar, _____ give to our/their daughter/son the English name _____, and the Hebrew name _____. May she/he live and grow in health and happiness.

On this day, we/they declare that we/they give to our/their daughter/son the name "Jew," and thus bring her/him into the community of Israel. May this name we now bestow from without come to have ever greater meaning within. May it resonate within the depths of her/his being, calling forth an authentic and enduring response.

Parents or Reader: May _____'s life be one of security and trust. *Yevarechecha adonai veyishmerecha.*

May _____'s life shine with dignity and freedom.
Ya-er adonai panav eilecha veechunecka.

May _____'s life know the creative harmony of peace.
Yisah adonai panav eilcha ve-yasem lecha shalom.

May we/you bring our/your daughter/son into the ways of Torah, chuppah, and ma-asim tovim, into the way of learning, the way of growth, capable of giving and receiving love, and concern for family and community, justice and healing. Amen.

THE PARENTS' DECLARATION (optional)

It is the way of parents to care for their children. Yet we would not protect you overmuch or overlong so that our love becomes a prison from which you must escape. As the poet has written:

Your children are not your children. They are the sons and
      daughters of Life's longing for itself.
They come through you but not from you, and though they are
      with you yet they belong not to you.
You may give them your love but not your thoughts, for they have
      their own thoughts.
You may house their bodies but not their souls, for their souls
      dwell in the house of tomorrow, which you cannot visit,
      not even in your dreams.
You may strive to be like them, but seek not to make them like you.
For life goes not backward nor tarries with yesterday.
You are the bows from which your children as living arrows are
      sent forth.
The archer sees the mark upon the path of the infinite, and He
      bends you with His might that His arrows may go swift
      and far.

Let your bending in the archer's hand be for gladness;
For even as He loves the arrow that flies, so He loves also the bow
   that is stable.*

It is in this spirit that today (_____ and) I declare to you:
   Your existence is your possession, not ours. Out of our
   love and concern we intrude in your life for a little while,
   to help you live and grow. It is our hope and our prayer
   that we will know when that time is done. For then, with
   grace and respect, we must return to you what has been
   ours only in trust, that which has always been rightfully
   yours: yourself.

You are not in this world to live up to my expectations.
   You are you
   And I am I.

Blessed are you my/our child in the newness of your existence.
Blessed are we who have been enriched by your life.†

* Kahlil Gibran, *The Prophet* (1923: reprint, New York: Alfred A. Knopf, 1991), 17.
† Sheldon Blank & Alvin Reines, "Ennomination Ceremony"; Anthony Holz,
   "Ennomination Ceremony."

Poems
Laurie Epstein

Invitation to a Bris

Please come to our house next Tuesday
    at 11 A.M. for a bris.

I cannot come, I reply.

Why?

I love you and your baby,
And I would love to welcome your baby
    at a gathering of loved ones.

But
    I cannot condone a tradition that causes pain;
    I cannot pretend that it does not matter or I do not care.
    It makes me feel queasy,
    And I must follow my conscience.

I will welcome your baby in another way.
I will congratulate you and share your joy.

So I repeat,

I will not come.

The Bris

Friends and relatives gather.
Mazel tov! you say.
You smile at the newborn baby.

Some of you feel queasy and go to another room
    so that you can't see or hear.

Pay attention! How do you feel?

It's over.
You stand around eating and talking.
Your uneasiness lingers.

Remember, each of you has helped to continue the tradition.

Why do you agree to attend such a "party"?

Invitation to an Alternative Bris

Please come to our house next Tuesday
     at 11 A.M. for an alternative bris.

I will be there, I reply.

I love you and your baby,
And I am delighted to share in a religious celebration
     that makes everyone, especially the baby, feel wonderful.

It is an honor to attend.

It is an honor to know people
Who have been true to their own conscience and their baby,
Who have the courage to interrupt a hurtful ancient tradition,
And replace it with a loving new one.

So I repeat,

I will be there.

The Alternative Bris

Friends and relatives gather
Mazel tov! you say
You smile at the newborn baby.

The rabbi, parents, or another person recites prayers
And welcomes the baby to his family, religious community,
    and the world.

Everyone remains to watch, listen, and participate.

When it is over, you share a festive meal and celebrate.

Do you realize, all of you have helped create a new joyful tradition,
    that may be passed on for many thousands of years?

How do you feel?

Proud.

Notes

Introduction

[1] Helliker, K., "Anxious Parents Question Merits of Circumcision," *Wall Street Journal*, 28 May 1996, A21; Wallerstein, E., "Circumcision: The Uniquely American Medical Enigma," *Symposium on Advances in Pediatric Urology, Urologic Clinics of North America* 12 (1985): 123-32.

[2] American Academy of Pediatrics, "Report of the Task Force on Circumcision," *Pediatrics* 84 (1989): 388–91.

[3] National Center for Health Statistics, telephone conversation with the author, 1995. Rate is for 1993.

[4] Silverman, J., "Circumcision: The Delicate Dilemma," *The Jewish Monthly*, November 1991, 31; Moss, L., "Circumcision: A Jewish Inquiry," *Midstream*, January 1992, 20–3; Katz. L., "Mitzvah or Mutilation? Circumcision Sparks Debate," *Northern California Jewish Bulletin*, 14 February 1992, 4.

[5] Eilberg-Schwartz, H., "A Masculine Critique of a Father God," *Tikkun*, September–October 1995, 61–2.

[6] Steinberg, M., *Basic Judaism* (rev. ed.) (New York: Harcourt Brace Jovanovich, 1975), 28.

[7] Maslin, S., *What We Believe, What We Do*, pamphlet, New York: UAHC Press, 1993.

[8] Borowitz, E., "The Concept of the Covenant in Reform Judaism," in L. Barth, ed., *Berit Mila in the Reform Context* (Berit Milah Board of Reform Judaism, 1990), 155.

[9] Union of American Hebrew Congregations, Programs and Services brochure, New York, August 1990, 2.

[10] Kosmin, B. et al., *Highlights of the CJF 1990 National Jewish Population Survey*, New York: Council of Jewish Federations, 1991, 28, 30.

Chapter 1 Origins and Background

[1] Eilberg-Schwartz, H., "Why Not the Earlobe?" *Moment*, February 1992, 32.

[2] *Midrash Tanchuma, Tazria* 5; *Bereishit Rabbah* 11:6.

[3] Montagu, A., *Sex, Man, & Society* (New York: G.P. Putnam's Sons, 1969).

[4] Greenberg, M., "Judaism," in *The New Encyclopedia Britannica* (Vol. 22) (Chicago: Encyclopedia Britannica, 1993), 381.

[5] Cain, S., "Bible," in *The New Encyclopedia Britannica* (Vol. 14) (Chicago: Encyclopedia Britannica, 1993), 922.

[6] Gevirtz, S., "Circumcision in the Biblical Period," in L. Barth, ed., *Berit Milah in the Reform Context* (Berit Milah Board of Reform Judaism, 1990), 97.

[7] Wine, S., "Circumcision," *Humanistic Judaism* 16 (Summer 1988): 6.

[8] Hoffman, L., *Covenant of Blood: Circumcision and Gender in Rabbinic Judaism* (Chicago: University of Chicago Press, 1996), 60–3.

[9] Ibid., 196.

[10] Morgenstern, J., *Rites of Birth, Marriage, Death and Kindred Occasions* (Cincinnati: Hebrew Union College Press, 1966), 63–5.

[11] Biale, D., quoted in S. Church, "Jewish Rite of Brit Milah: Giving Thanks for a Birth," *Binghamton (NY) Press SunBulletin*, 27 April 1986.

[12] Chyet, S. & Mirsky, N., "Reflections on Circumcision as Sacrifice," in L. Barth, ed., *Berit Mila in the Reform Context* (Berit Milah Board of Reform Judaism, 1990), 61.

[13] Eilberg-Schwartz, "Why Not the Earlobe?" 28–33.

[14] Lewis, J., *In the Name of Humanity* (New York: Eugenics Publishing, 1949), 26.

[15] Eilberg-Schwartz, "Why Not the Earlobe?" 33.

[16] Walker, B., *The Crone: Woman of Age, Wisdom, and Power* (San Francisco: Harper Collins, 1985), 47–8.

[17] Glasner, S., letter to the editor, *Fact*, Oct. 1966.

[18] Beidelman, T., *The Encyclopedia of Religion* (Vol. 3) (MacMillan Publishing: New York, 1987), 511.

[19] Eilberg-Schwartz, "Why Not the Earlobe?" 28; Biale in "Jewish Rite of Brit Milah."

[20] Brown, M. & Brown, C., "Circumcision Decision: Prominence of Social Concerns," *Pediatrics* 80 (1987): 219.

[21] Schacter-Shalomi, Z., *The First Step* (New York: Bantam, 1983), 103.

[22] Hall, R., "Epispasm: Circumcision in Reverse," *Moment*, February 1992, 34–7; Jubilees 15: 33–4.

[23] "Circumcision," in *Encyclopedia Judaica* (Vol. 5) (Jerusalem: Keter Publishing, 1971), 570.

[24] Meyer, M., *Response to Modernity: A History of the Reform Movement in Judaism* (New York: Oxford University Press, 1988), 123.

[25] Meyer, M., "Berit Milah within the History of the Reform Movement," in L. Barth, ed., *Berit Mila in the Reform Context*, (Berit Milah Board of Reform Judaism, 1990), 144.

[26] Ibid., 144.

[27] Philipson, *The Reform Movement in Judaism*, 136.

[28] Ibid., 137.

[29] Ibid., 280.

[30] Meyer, "Berit Milah within the History of the Reform Movement," 146.

[31] Meyer, *Response to Modernity: A History of the Reform Movement in Judaism*, 163.

[32] Ibid., 166.

[33] Meyer, "Berit Milah within the History of the Reform Movement," 144.

[34] Ibid.

[35] Stewart, D., *Theordor Herzl* (Garden City, NY: Doubleday, 1974), 202.

[36] Karsenty, N., "A Mother Questions Brit Milla," *Humanistic Judaism* 16 (Summer 1988), 21.

[37] Israeli, no permission to disclose name, telephone conversation with author, 1995.

[38] Wallerstein, E., *Circumcision: An American Health Fallacy* (New York: Springer Publishing, 1980), 158; Hall, R., "Epispasm: Circumcision in Reverse," *Moment*, February 1992, 34–7.

[39] Hall, "Epispasm: Circumcision in Reverse," 34–7.

[40] Wallerstein, *Circumcision: An American Health Fallacy*, 158.

[41] No permission to disclose name, telephone conversation with author, 1995.

Chapter 2 Assumed Benefits

[1] Roth, J., "The Meaning for Today," *Moment*, February 1992, 43.

[2] Kushner, M., "Ancient Ritual is Beneficial," *(Philadelphia) Jewish Times*, 21 March 1991, 30.

[3] Roth, "The Meaning for Today," 44.

[4] Kosmin et al., *Jewish Population Survey*, 14.

[5] "Circumcision," in *Encyclopedia Judaica* (Vol. 5) (Jerusalem: Keter Publishing, 1971), 570.

[6] Altmann, A., "Circumcision Questions," letter to the editor, *Northern California Jewish Bulletin*, 31 May 1985, 12.

[7] Ruby, W., "Reform vs. Conservative: Who's Winning?" *Moment* April 1996, 32, 37.

[8] Sherif, M., "Conformity-Deviation, Norms, and Group Relations," in I. Berg & B. Bass, eds., *Conformity and Deviation* (New York: Harper, 1961), 59–181; Keating, J. & Brock, T., "Acceptance of Persuasion and the Inhibition of Counterargument under Various Distraction Tasks," *Journal of Experimental Social Psychology* 10 (1974): 301–9; Luchins, A., "Focusing on the Object of Judgment in the Social Situation," *Journal of Social Psychology* 60 (1963): 231–49.

[9] Milgram, S., "Group Pressure and Action against a Person," *Journal of Abnormal and Social Psychology* 69 (1964): 137–43; Gerald, H., Wilhelm, R., & Conelley, E., "Conformity and Group Size," Journal of Personality and Social Psychology 8 (1968): 79–82.

[10] Wiswell, T., Smith, F., & Bass, J., "Decreased Incidence of Urinary Tract Infections in Circumcised Male Infants," *Pediatrics* 75 (1985): 901–3; Wiswell, T. et al., "Declining Frequency of Circumcision: Implications for Changes in the Absolute Incidence and Male to Female Sex Ratio of Urinary Tract Infection in Early Infancy," *Pediatrics* 79 (1987): 338–42.

[11] American Academy of Pediatrics, "Task Force on Circumcision," 389.

[12] Altschul, M., "Cultural Bias and the Urinary Tract Infection (UTI) Circumcision Controversy," *The Truth Seeker*, July/August 1989, 43–5.

[13] Wiswell, Smith, & Bass, "Decreased Incidence," 901–3; Wiswell et al., "Declining Frequency," 338–42.

[14] Kaplan, G., "Complications of Circumcision," *Urological Clinics of North America* 10 (1983): 543–9; Gee, W. & Ansell, J., "Neonatal Circumcision: A Ten Year Overview with Comparison of the Gomco Clamp and the Plastibell Device," *Pediatrics* 58 (1976): 824–7.

[15] Kaweblum, Y. et al., "Circumcision Using the Mogen Clamp," *Clinical Pediatrics* 23 (1984): 679–82.

[16] Denniston, G., "First, Do No Harm," *The Truth Seeker*, July/August 1989, 35–8.

[17] Wiswell et al., "Declining Frequency," 338–42.

[18] American Academy of Pediatrics, "Task Force on Circumcision," 389.

[19] American Academy of Pediatrics, *Newborns: Care of the Uncircumcised Penis* (pamphlet for parents), Elk Grove Village, IL: author, 1992.

[20] Wallerstein, *Circumcision: An American Health Fallacy*, 128.

[21] Ibid.

[22] Romberg, R., *Circumcision: The Painful Dilemma* (South Hadley, MA: Bergin & Garvey, 1985), 235–76.

[23] Spock, B., *The Common Sense Book of Baby and Child Care* (New York: Duell, Sloan, and Pearce, 1946), 18; Spock, B. & Rothenberg, M., *Dr. Spock's Baby and Child Care* (New York: Pocket Books, 1992), 227.

[24] Wallerstein, *Circumcision: An American Health Fallacy*, 163.

[25] Singer, S., "The Pain and the Pleasure," *Moment*, February 1992, 38–40.

[26] Errors included inflated American circumcision rate, penile cancer rate, and adult circumcision rate. Complications and infant behavioral changes after circumcision were among omitted items. The opinions of Aaron Fink, which conflict with the latest research, were stated at length without response.

[27] Goldenberg, T., "Medical Issues and Berit Milah," in L. Barth, ed., *Berit Mila in the Reform Context* (Berit Mila Board of Reform Judaism, 1990).

[28] Festinger, L. & Carlsmith, J., "Cognitive Consequences of Forced Compliance," *Journal of Abnormal and Social Psychology* 58 (1959): 203–10.

Chapter 3 Risks: Opinion versus Research

[1] Weiss, R., quoted in S. Church, "Jewish Rite of Brit Milah: Giving Thanks for a Birth," *Binghamton (NY) Press & SunBulletin*, 27 April 1986.

[2] Raul-Friedman, E., "A Rebuttal—Circumcision: A Jewish Legacy," *Midstream*, May 1992, 31.

[3] Landis, D. & Robbin, S., "Gainful Pain," *Tikkun*, Sept/Oct 1990, 74.

[4] Berlin, S., "From the Jewish Journal: Don't Fear Brit Milah," *Berit Milah Newsletter*, 6 Oct. 1989, 6.

[5] Romirowsky, S., "Psycho-Social Aspects of Brit Milah," *Conservative Judaism*, Summer 1990, 42.

[6] Cohen, E., letter to the editor, *New York Times*, 25 May 1996, A18.

[7] Meyers, A., "Newborns Feel Pain," letter to the editor, *New York Times*, 29 May 1996, A18.

[8] Anand, K. & Hickey, P., "Pain and Its Effects in the Human Neonate and Fetus," *New England Journal of Medicine* 317 (1987): 1326.

[9] Owens, M., & Todt, E., "Pain in Infancy: Neonatal Reaction to a Heel Lance," *Pain* 20 (1984): 77–86; Craig, K. et al., "Pain in the Preterm Neonate: Behavioral and Physiological Indices," *Pain* 52 (1993): 287–99.

[10] Craig, K., Hadjistavropoulos, H., & Grunau, R., "A Comparison of Two Measures of Facial Activity during Pain in the Newborn Child," *Journal of Pediatric Psychology* 19 (1994): 305–18; Grunau, R., Johnston, C., & Craig, K., "Neonatal Facial and Cry Responses to Invasive and Non-Invasive Procedures," *Pain* 42 (1990): 295–305.

[11] Grunau, R. & Craig, K., "Pain Expression in Neonates: Facial Action and Cry," *Pain* 28 (1987): 395–410; Markessinis, J., *The First Week of Life* (Princeton, NJ: Edcom Systems, 1971), 23; Sherman, M. & Sherman, I., "Sensori-Motor Responses in Infants," *Journal of Comparative Psychology* 5 (1925): 53–68.

[12] Gunnar, M. et al., "Adrenocortical Activity and Behavioral Distress in Human Newborns," *Developmental Psychobiology* 21 (1988): 297–310; Malone, S., Gunnar, M., & Fisch, R., "Adrenocortical and Behavioral Responses to Limb Restraint in Human Neonates," *Developmental Psychobiology* 18 (1985): 435–46.

[13] Ryan, C. & Finer, N., "Changing Attitudes and Practices Regarding Local Analgesia for Newborn Circumcision," *Pediatrics* 94 (1994): 232.

[14] Howard, C., Howard, F., & Weitzman, M., "Acetaminophen Analgesis in Neonatal Circumcision: The Effect on Pain," *Pediatrics* 93 (1994): 645.

[15] Benini, F. et al., "Topical Anesthesia during Circumcision in Newborn Infants," *Journal of the American Medical Association* 270 (1993): 850–3.

[16] Gunnar, M. et al., "Coping with Aversive Stimulation in the Neonatal Period: Quiet Sleep and Plasma Cortisol Levels during Recovery from Circumcision," *Child Development* 56 (1985): 824–34.

[17] Williamson, P. & Williamson, M., "Physiologic Stress Reduction by a Local Anesthetic during Newborn Circumcision," *Pediatrics* 71 (1983): 40.

[18] Stang, H. et al., "Local Anesthesia for Neonatal Circumcision," *Journal of the American Medical Association* 259 (1988): 1510.

[19] Porter, F., Miller, R., & Marshall, R., "Neonatal Pain Cries: Effect of Circumcision on Acoustic Features and Perceived Urgency," *Child Development* 57 (1986): 790.

[20] Zeskind, P., & Marshall, T., "The Relation between Variations in Pitch and Maternal Perceptions of Infant Crying," *Child Development* 59 (1988): 193–6.

[21] Connelly, K., Shropshire, L., & Salzberg, A., "Gastric Rupture Associated with Prolonged Crying in a Newborn Undergoing Circumcision," *Clinical Pediatrics* 31 (1992): 560–1.

[22] Gunnar, M., Fisch, R., & Malone, S., "The Effects of a Pacifying Stimulus on Behavioral and Adrenocortical Responses to Circumcision in the Newborn," *Journal of the American Academy of Child Psychiatry* 23 (1984): 34–8.

[23] Brazelton, T., *Doctor and Child* (New York: Delacorte Press, 1976), 31; Ostwald, P. & Peltzman, P., "The Cry of the Human Infant," *Scientific American* 230 (1974): 85.

[24] Call, J., quoted in R. Romberg, *Circumcision: The Painful Dilemma*, 321.

[25] Brooks, T., quoted in R. Romberg, *Circumcision: The Painful Dilemma*, 325.

[26] Roberts, M., "Shear Bris," *Denver Westword*, 24 February 1993, 29.

[27] Ibid., 24.

[28] Milos, M., "Infant Circumcision: 'What I Wish I Had Known,'" *The Truth Seeker* (July/August 1989): 3.

[29] Schultz, T., "A Nurse's View on Circumcision," *Circumcision: The Rest of the Story* (Santa Fe, NM: Mothering, 1993), 80-1.

[30] Ryan & Finer, "Changing Attitudes and Practices," 230–3.

[31] Stang et al., "Local Anesthesia for Neonatal Circumcision," 1507–11.

[32] Rabinowitz, R. & Hulbert, W., "Newborn Circumcision Should Not Be Performed without Anesthesia," *Birth* 22 (1995): 45–6.

[33] Schechter, N., "The Undertreatment of Pain in Children: An Overview," *Pediatric Clinics of North America* 36 (1989): 781–94.

[34] Wallerstein, *Circumcision: An American Health Fallacy*, 158; Romberg, H., *Bris Milah* (New York: Feldheim, 1982), 41.

[35] "Circumcision," in *Encyclopedia Judaica*, 572; Krohn, P., *Bris Milah* (Brooklyn: Mesorah Publishing, 1985), 99.

[36] Wallerstein, *Circumcision: An American Health Fallacy*, 158; "Circumcision," in *Encyclopedia Judaica*, 572; Romberg, *Bris Milah*, 58.

[37] Porter, Miller, & Marshall, "Neonatal Pain Cries: Effect of Circumcision on Acoustic Features and Perceived Urgency," 790–802.

[38] Paige, K., "The Ritual of Circumcision," *Human Nature*, May 1978, 42; Anders, T. & Chalemian, R., "The Effects of Circumcision on Sleep-Wake States in Human Neonates," *Psychosomatic Medicine* 36 (1974): 174–9; Brackbill, Y., "Continuous Stimulation and Arousal Level in Infancy: Effects of Stimulus Intensity and Stress," *Child Development* 46 (1975): 364–9.

[39] Marshall, R. et al., "Circumcision: II. Effects upon Mother-Infant Interaction," *Early Human Development* 7 (1982): 367–74.

[40] Howard, Howard, & Weitzman, "Acetaminophen Analgesis in Neonatal Circumcision: The Effect on Pain."

[41] Dixon, S. et al., "Behavioral Effects of Circumcision with and without Anesthesia," *Journal of Development and Behavioral Pediatrics* 5 (1984): 246–50.

[42] American Academy of Pediatrics, "Report of the Task Force on Circumcision," 388-91.

[43] Richards, M., Bernal, J., & Brackbill, Y. "Early Behavioral Differences: Gender or Circumcision?" *Developmental Psychobiology* 9 (1976): 93.

[44] Marshall, R. et al., "Circumcision: I. Effects upon Newborn Behavior," *Infant Behavior and Development* 3 (1980): 1–14.

[45] Telephone conversation with the author, 1994.

[46] Anand & Hickey, "Pain and Its Effects," 1325.

[47] Walco, G., Cassidy, R., & Schechter, N., "Pain, Hurt, and Harm," *New England Journal of Medicine* 331 (1994): 542.

[48] Taddio, A. et al., "Effect of Neonatal Circumcision on Pain Response during Subsequent Routine Vaccination," *The Lancet* 349 (1997): 599–603; Taddio, A. et al., "Effect of Neonatal Circumcision on Pain Responses during Vaccination of Boys," *The Lancet* 345 (1995): 291–2.

[49] American Psychiatric Association, *Diagnostic and Statistical Manual of Mental Disorders*, 4th ed., (Washington, DC: author, 1994), 424.

[50] Wilson, J., *Trauma, Transformation, and Healing*, (New York: Brunner/ Mazel, 1989), 201.

[51] American Psychiatric Association, *Diagnostic and Statistical Manual*, 426.

[52] Schacter-Shalomi, Z., *The First Step*, 103.

[53] Kaplan, G., "Complications of Circumcision," *Urological Clinics of North America* 10 (1983): 543-9; Gee, W. & Ansell, J., "Neonatal Circumcision: A Ten Year Overview with Comparison of the Gomco Clamp and the Plasti-bell Device," *Pediatrics* 58 (1976): 824-7.

[54] Kaweblum, Y. et al., "Circumcision Using the Mogen Clamp," *Clinical Pediatrics* 23 (1984): 679-82.

[55] "Circumcision," in *Encyclopedia Judaica*, 572; Sh.Ar., YD 263:2-3.

Chapter 4 Unrecognized Consequences

[1] Landis & Robbin, "Gainful Pain," 73.

[2] Krohn, *Bris Milah*, 29, 69, 121, 126.

[3] Gevirtz, "Circumcision in the Biblical Period," 125.

[4] "Circumcision," in *Encyclopedia Judaica*, 574

[5] Hall, "Epispasm: Circumcision in Reverse," 36.

[6] Schacter-Shalomi, *The First Step*, 102.

[7] Maimonides, M., *Guide for the Perplexed* (1190: reprint, New York: Dover Publications, 1956), 378.

[8] Taylor, J., Lockwood, A., & Taylor, A., "The Prepuce: Specialized Mucosa of the Penis and Its Loss to Circumcision," *British Journal of Urology* 77 (1996): 294

[9] Ibid., 292, 294.

[10] Ibid., 295.

[11] Ritter, T., *Say No to Circumcision* (Aptos, CA: Hourglass, 1992): 18-1; Morgan, W., "The Rape of the Phallus," *Journal of the American Medical Association* 193 (1965): 223–4.

[12] Bigelow, J., *The Joy of Uncircumcising!* (Aptos, CA: Hourglass, 1995), 17; Denniston, G., "Unnecessary Circumcision," *The Female Patient* 17 (1992): 13–14; Ritter, *Say No to Circumcision*, 6-2.

[13] Ritter, *Say No To Circumcision*, 11-1.

[14] Money, J. & Davison, J., "Adult Penile Circumcision: Erotosexual and Cosmetic Sequelae," *Journal of Sex Research* 19 (1983): 291.

[15] Milos, M. & Macris, D., "Circumcision: A Medical or a Human Rights Issue?" *Journal of Nurse-Midwifery* 37 (Supplement 1992): 93S.

[16] No permission to disclose name, telephone conversation with the author, 1993.

[17] NOCIRC Newsletter, Fall 1990, 3.

[18] "The Unkindest Cut of All," letter to the editor, *Playgirl*, July 1979, 108.

[19] Edell, D., Circumcision report for television news, KGO, San Francisco, 1984.

[20] Newman, R., "Circumcision: The False Initiation," *Changing Men*, Fall/Winter 1991, 19–21.

[21] Hammond, T., *Awakenings: A Preliminary Poll of Circumcised Males* (San Francisco: NOHARMM, 1994), A9-A30.

[22] Warren, J., et al., "Circumcision of Children," *British Medical Journal* 312 (1996): 377.

[23] Terr, L., "What Happens to Early Memories of Trauma?" *Journal of the American Academy of Child and Adolescent Psychiatry* 27 (1988): 96–104; van der Kolk, B., "The Compulsion to Repeat the Trauma: Re-Enactment, Revictimization, and Masochism," *Psychiatric Clinics of North America* 12 (1989): 389–411.

[24] Terr, L., "Childhood Traumas: An Outline and Overview," *American Journal of Psychiatry* 148 (1991): 14.

Chapter 5 Personal Experiences

[1] Silverman, J., "Circumcision: The Delicate Dilemma," *The Jewish Monthly*, November 1991, 31.

[2] Meyer, M., "Berit Milah within the History of the Reform Movement," in L. Barth, ed., *Berit Mila in the Reform Context* (Berit Milah Board of Reform Judaism 1990), 149.

[3] Schacter-Shalomi, Z., *The First Step*, 98.

[4] Ibid., 99.

[5] Ibid., 104; telephone conversation with the author, 1997.

[6] Bivas, N., letter to the author, 1991.

[7] Frodi, A. & Lamb, M., "Sex Differences in Responsiveness to Infants: A Developmental Study of Psychophysical and Behavioral Responses," *Child Development* 49 (1978): 1182–8.

[8] O'Mara, P., ed., *Circumcision: The Rest of the Story* (Santa Fe, NM: *Mothering*, 1993), 75–6.

[9] Friederich, L., letter in O'Mara, *Circumcision: The Rest of the Story*, 79.

[10] Pollack, M., "Circumcision: A Jewish Feminist Perspective," in K. Weiner & A. Moon, eds., *Jewish Women Speak Out* (Seattle, WA: Canopy Press, 1995), 172; Conversation with the author, College Park, MD, May 1994.

[11] Interview with the author, Needham, MA, 1994.

[12] Romberg, *Circumcision: The Painful Dilemma*, 78–84.

[13] Sexty, L., letter in O'Mara, *Circumcision: The Rest of the Story*, 84.

[14] Cohen, N., interview with the author, Needham, MA, 1994.

[15] A father as quoted by Northrup, C., telephone conversation with the author, 1994.

[16] Raisbeck, B., "Circumcision: A Wound Which Lasts a Lifetime," *Healing Currents*, 1993, 21.

[17] Schonfeld, V., "First Cut is the Unkindest," *The Guardian*, 20 September 1995, 5.

[18] Bigony, D., letter to the author, 1994.

[19] Cohen, N., interview with the author, 1994.

[20] Pollack, M., telephone conversation with the author, 1997.

[21] Circumcision, in *Encyclopedia Judaica*, 571.

[22] Silverman, "Circumcision: The Delicate Dilemma," 32.

[23] Bivas, N., letter to the author, 1991.

[24] Bivas, "Letter to Our Son's Grandparents," 13.

[25] Schonfeld, V., "It's a Boy," documentary on circumcision, Ch. 4, England, 21 Sept. 1995.

[26] Shulman, A., letter to the author, 1991.

[27] Paisner, J., conversation with the author, 1992.

[28] Ginzburg, R., "Is Circumcision Indefensible?" letter to the editor, *New York Times Book Review*, 13 May 1990.

[29] Rothenberg, M., telephone conversation with the author, 1991.

[30] Parmes-Katz, D., telephone conversations with the author, 1994.

[31] Schulz, Z., conversation with the author, 1994.

[32] Felshman, J., "The Foreskin Flap: Is Circumcision Really Worth It?" *Chicago Reader,* 10 March 1995, 17.

[33] Newman, L., telephone conversation with the author, 1997.

Chapter 6 Conflicts and Questions

[1] Moss, L., "Circumcision: A Jewish Inquiry," *Midstream,* January 1992, 20–1.

[2] Pollack, M., "Circumcision: A Jewish Feminist Perspective," in K. Weiner & A. Moon, eds., *Jewish Women Speak Out*, (Seattle, WA: Canopy Press, 1995), 182.

[3] Steinberg, *Basic Judaism*, 35.

[4] Borowitz, E., "The Concept of the Covenant in Reform Judaism," in L. Barth, ed., *Berit Mila in the Reform Context* (Berit Milah Board of Reform Judaism, 1990), 160.

[5] Steinberg, *Basic Judaism*, 35.

[6] Donin, H., *To Be a Jew* (New York: Basic Books, 1972), 56.

[7] Philipson, *The Reform Movement in Judaism*, 371–2.

[8] Goldman, R., *Circumcision: The Hidden Trauma* (Boston: Vanguard Publications, 1997), 6–28.

[9] Romberg, R., "Circumcision Feedback," letter to the editor, *Mensa Bulletin*, May 1993.

[10] Maimonides, M., *Mishneh Torah, Hilchot Rotze'ach* 2:6.

[11] Cantor, A., *Jewish Women, Jewish Men* (San Francisco: Harper Collins, 1995), jacket notes.

[12] Kramer, W., "Denial of Spousal Abuse the Jewish Problem," *Jewish Spectator* (1994, fall), 6; Arnold, M., "Domestic Violence Coming into Focus in Israel," *Forward*, 29 Nov. 1996, 1; "Shattering the Myth: Developing an Orthodox Response to Domestic Violence," *The Jewish Advocate*, 20-26 Dec. 1996, 33.

[13] *Pirke Avot*, I, 5.

[14] Hauptman, J., "Images of Women in the Talmud," in R. Ruether, ed., *Religion and Sexism: Images of Women in Jewish and Christian Traditions* (New York: Simon and Schuster, 1974), 207.

[15] Hoffman, *Covenant of Blood*, 22.

[16] Ibid., 156.

[17] Erikson, E., *Childhood and Society* (New York: Norton, 1963), 249.

[18] Laibow, R., "Circumcision and Its Relationship to Attachment Impairment," in *Syllabus of Abstracts*, The Second International Symposium on Circumcision, San Francisco, 1991, 14.

[19] van der Kolk, B., *Psychological Trauma* (Washington, DC: American Psychiatric Press, 1987), 35.

[20] Hartman, C. & Burgess, A., "Information Processing of Trauma," *Child Abuse and Neglect* 17 (1993): 47–58.

[21] Kennedy, H., "Trauma in Childhood: Signs and Sequelae as Seen in the Analysis of an Adolescent," *Psychoanalytic Study of the Child* 41 (1986): 209–19.

[22] Cansever, G., "Psychological Effects of Circumcision," *British Journal of Medical Psychology* 38 (1965): 328.

Chapter 7 Preventing More Pain

[1] Bivas, N., letter to the author, 1991; Shulman, A., letter to the author, 1991.

[2] Schacter-Shalomi, Z., letter to the author, 1990.

[3] Hoffman, *Covenant of Blood*, 218.

[4] Goodman, J., "We're Made in God's Image So Why Change Perfection?" *Independent*, 21 Sept. 1995, section two.

[5] Schonfeld, V. & Bard, J., "Severing the Chain," *The Jewish Quarterly*, winter 1995, 27–31.

[6] Goodman, J., telephone conversation with the author, 24 Sept. 1995.

[7] Romain, J., "Keeping the Faith," *Jewish Chronicle*, 23 Feb. 1996, 28.

[8] Kushner, L., *The River of Light* (San Francisco: Harper & Row, 1981), 60.

[9] Amsel, N., "Meaning of Brit Milah," *The Jewish Encyclopedia of Moral and Ethical Issues* (Northvale, NJ: Jason Aronson, 1994), 157.

[10] Scott, L., "The Unkindest Cut? Opponents of Circumcision Question Necessity of Jewish Rite," *The Jewish Community Voice*, 30 August 1995, 9–10.

[11] Editorial, "Shame on TVO," *Canadian Jewish News*, 17 October 1996, 8.

[12] Goldman, *Circumcision: The Hidden Trauma*, 103–23.

[13] Pickard-Ginsburg, M., "Jesse's Circumcision," *Mothering*, Spring 1979, 6.

[14] Pugh, L., "Santa Fe Nurses Rejects Circumcisions," *Albuquerque Journal*, 13 June 1995, 1.

[15] Gillie, O., "Doctors, Spare That Foreskin," *Independent*, 7 April 1996, 8.

[16] Steinberg, J., "Government Wants Community to Justify Ritual Circumcision," *Australian Jewish News, Queensland Edition*, 28 January 1994, 1.

[17] Rothenberg, M., letter to the author, 1988.

[18] Ritter, *Say No to Circumcision*, 12-1.

[19] Goldman, *Circumcision: The Hidden Trauma*, 103–23.

[20] Bivas, N., telephone conversation with the author, 1994.

[21] Susskind, J., "Circumcision is Cruel and Harmful," letter to the editor, *Moment*, June 1992, 7.

Appendix E Circumcision and Anti-Semitism

[1] Schäfer, P., *Judeophobia: Attitudes toward the Jews in the Ancient World* (Cambridge, MA: Harvard University Press, 1997).

[2] Weill, T., "Anti-Semitism: Selected Psychodynamic Insights," *American Journal of Psychoanalysis* 41 (1981): 142.

[3] Loewenstein, R., *Christians and Jews: A Psychoanalytic Study* (New York: International Universities Press, 1951), 34.

[4] Gilbert, G., *Nuremberg Diary* (New York: Farrar, Straus and Company, 1947), 10, 41, 125.

[5] Loewenstein, R., *Christians and Jews: A Psychoanalytic Study* (New York: International Universities Press, 1951), 72.

[6] Freud, S., *Moses and Monotheism*, v. 23. (London: Hogarth, 1939); Loewenstein, R., *Christians and Jews: A Psychoanalytic Study* (New York: International Universities Press, 1951); Fenichel, O., "Elements of a Psychoanalytic

Theory of Anti-Semitism." In E. Simmel, ed., *Anti-Semitism, A Social Disease* (New York: International Universities Press, 1946).

[7] Allport, G., *The Nature of Prejudice* (Cambridge, MA: Addison-Wesley, 1954), 248.

Appendix G Alternative Rituals

[1] Cohen, E., *Guide to Ritual Circumcision and Redemption of the First-Born Son* (New York: Ktav Publishers, 1984), xiii.

[2] Roth, J., "The Meaning for Today," *Moment*, February 1992, 43.

[3] Ibid., 43.

[4] Hosken, F., *The Hosken Report*, Lexington, MA: Women's International Network News, 1993.

Bibliography

Altmann, A. "Circumcision Questions," letter to the editor. *Northern California Jewish Bulletin*, 31 May 1985, 12.

Altschul, M. "Cultural Bias and the Urinary Tract Infection (UTI) Circumcision Controversy." *The Truth Seeker*, July/August 1989, 43–5.

American Academy of Pediatrics. "Report of the Task Force on Circumcision." *Pediatrics* 84 (1989): 388–91.

American Academy of Pediatrics, *Newborns: Care of the Uncircumcised Penis* (pamphlet for parents), Elk Grove Village, IL: author, 1992.

American Psychiatric Association. *Diagnostic and Statistical Manual of Mental Disorders*, 4th ed. Washington, DC: author, 1994.

*Amsel, N. "Meaning of Bit Milah." *The Jewish Encyclopedia of Moral and Ethical Issues*. Northvale, NJ: Jason Aronson, 1994.

Anand, K. & Hickey, P. "Pain and Its Effects in the Human Neonate and Fetus." *New England Journal of Medicine* 317 (1987): 1321–9.

Anders, T. & Chalemian, R. "The Effects of Circumcision on Sleep-Wake States in Human Neonates," *Psychosomatic Medicine* 36 (1974): 174–9.

Arnold, M. "Domestic Violence Coming into Focus in Israel." *Forward*, 29 Nov. 1996, 1.

Ballonoff, N. Quoted in N. Joseph, "Rabbi's Wife Sues to Block Future Britot." *Northern California Jewish Bulletin*, 26 April 1985, 35.

*Barth, L., ed. *Berit Mila in the Reform Context*. Berit Mila Board of Reform Judaism, 1990.

Beidelman, T., *The Encyclopedia of Religion* (Vol. 3) (MacMillan Publishing: New York, 1987), 511.

Benini, F., Johnson, C., Faucher, D., & Aranda, J. "Topical Anesthesia during Circumcision in Newborn Infants," *Journal of the American Medical Association* 270 (1993): 850–3.

*Berlin, S. "From the Jewish Journal: Don't Fear Brit Milah." *Berit Milah Newsletter*. Berit Milah Board of Reform Judaism, 6 Oct. 1989.

Biale, D. Quoted in S. Church, "Jewish Rite of Brit Milah: Giving Thanks for a Birth." *Binghamton (NY) Press SunBulletin*, 27 April 1986.

Bigelow, J. *The Joy of Uncircumcising*. Aptos, CA: Hourglass, 1992.

Bivas, N. "Letter to Our Son's Grandparents: Why We Decided against Circumcision." *Humanistic Judaism* 16 (1988, summer): 11–3.

*Borowitz, E. "The Concept of the Covenant in Reform Judaism." In L. Barth, ed., *Berit Mila in the Reform Context*. Berit Milah Board of Reform Judaism, 1990.

---

* Sources with an asterisk support circumcision. Most sources take no position.

Brackbill, Y. "Continuous Stimulation and Arousal Level in Infancy: Effects of Stimulus Intensity and Stress." *Child Development* 46 (1975): 364–9.

Brazelton, T. *Doctor and Child.* New York: Delacorte Press, 1976.

Brooks, T. Quoted in R. Romberg, *Circumcision: The Painful Dilemma.* South Hadley, MA: Bergin & Garvey, 1985.

Brown, M. & Brown, C. "Circumcision Decision: Prominence of Social Concerns." *Pediatrics* 80 (1987): 215–9.

Burns, N. "Alternative Bris." *Circumcision: The Rest of the Story.* Santa Fe, NM: Mothering, 1994.

Cain, S. "Bible." In *The New Encyclopedia Britannica* (Vol. 14). Chicago: Encyclopedia Britannica, 1993.

Call, J. Quoted in R. Romberg, *Circumcision: The Painful Dilemma.* South Hadley, MA: Bergin & Garvey, 1985.

Cansever, G. "Psychological Effects of Circumcision." *British Journal of Medical Psychology* 38 (1965): 328.

Cantor, A. *Jewish Women, Jewish Men.* San Francisco: Harper Collins, 1995.

*Chyet, S. & Mirsky, N. "Reflections on Circumcision as Sacrifice." In L. Barth, ed., *Berit mila in the Reform context.* Berit Milah Board of Reform Judaism, 1990.

*Circumcision. In *Encyclopedia Judaica* (Vol. 5). Jerusalem: Keter Publishing, 1971.

*Cohen, E. *Guide to Ritual Circumcision and Redemption of the First-Born Son.* New York: Ktav Publishers, 1984.

*Cohen, E. Letter to the editor. *New York Times*, 25 May 1996, 18.

Connelly, K., Shropshire, L., & Salzberg, A. "Gastric Rupture Associated with Prolonged Crying in a Newborn Undergoing Circumcision." *Clinical Pediatrics* 31 (1992): 560–1.

Craig, K., Hadjistavropoulos, H., & Grunau, R. "A Comparison of Two Measures of Facial Activity during Pain in the Newborn Child." *Journal of Pediatric Psychology* 19 (1994): 305–18.

Craig, K., Whitfield, M., Grunau, R., & Linton, J. "Pain in the Preterm Neonate: Behavioral and Physiological Indices," *Pain* 52 (1993): 287–99.

Denniston, G. "First, Do No Harm." *The Truth Seeker,* July/August 1989, 35–8.

Denniston, G. "Unnecessary Circumcision." *The Female Patient* 17 (1992): 13–4.

Dixon, S., Snyder, J., Holve, R., & Bromberger, P. "Behavioral Effects of Circumcision with and without Anesthesia," *Journal of Development and Behavioral Pediatrics* 5 (1984): 246–50.

*Donin, H. *To Be a Jew.* New York: Basic Books, 1972.

Edell, D. Circumcision report for television news. KGO. San Francisco, 1984.

*Editorial. "Shame on TVO." *Canadian Jewish News,* 17 October 1996, 8.

Eilberg-Schwartz, H. "Why Not the Earlobe?" *Moment,* February 1992, 28-33.

Eilberg-Schwaratz, H. "A Masculine Critique of a Father God." *Tikkun,* September-October, 1995, 58–62.

Erikson, E. *Childhood and Society.* New York: Norton, 1963.

Fenichel, O. "Elements of a Psychoanalytic Theory of Anti-Semitism." In E. Simmel, ed., *Anti-Semitism, A Social Disease*. New York: International Universities Press, 1946.

Festinger, L. & Carlsmith, J. "Cognitive Consequences of Forced Compliance." *Journal of Abnormal and Social Psychology* 58 (1959): 203–10.

Freud, S. *Moses and Monotheism*, vol. 23. London: Hogarth, 1939.

Frodi, A. & Lamb, M. "Sex Differences in Responsiveness to Infants: A Developmental Study of Psychophysical and Behavioral Responses." *Child Development* 49 (1978): 1182–8.

Friederich, L. Letter to the editor. In P. O'Mara, ed., *Circumcision: The Rest of the Story*. Santa Fe, NM: Mothering, 1993.

Gee, W. & Ansell, J. "Neonatal Circumcision: A Ten Year Overview with Comparison of the Gomco Clamp and the Plastibell Device," *Pediatrics* 58 (1976): 824–7.

Gerald, H., Wilhelm, R., & Conelley, E. "Conformity and Group Size." *Journal of Personality and Social Psychology* 8 (1968): 79–82.

*Gevirtz, S. "Circumcision in the Biblical Period." In L. Barth, ed., *Berit Milah in the Reform Context*. Berit Milah Board of Reform Judaism, 1990.

Gillie, O. "Doctors, Spare That Foreskin." *Independent*, 7 April 1996, 8

Gilbert, G. *Nuremberg Diary*. New York: Farrar, Straus and Company, 1947.

Ginzburg, R. "Is Circumcision Indefensible?" letter to the editor. *New York Times Book Review.* 13 May 1990.

Glasner, S. Letter to the editor. *Fact.* October 1966.

*Goldenberg, T. "Medical Issues and Berit Milah." In L. Barth, ed., *Berit Mila in the Reform Context*. Berit Mila Board of Reform Judaism, 1990.

Goldman, R. *Circumcision: The Hidden Trauma; How an American Cultural Practice Affects Infants and Ultimately Us All.* Boston: Vanguard Publications, 1997.

Goodman, J. "We're Made in God's Image So Why Change Perfection?" *Independent*, 21 Sept. 1995, section two.

Greenberg, M. "Judaism." In *The New Encyclopedia Britannica* (Vol. 22). Chicago: Encyclopedia Britannica, 1993.

Grunau, R., Johnston, C., & Craig, K. "Neonatal Facial and Cry Responses to Invasive and Non-Invasive Procedures." *Pain* 42 (1990): 295–305.

Grunau, R. & Craig, K. "Pain Expression in Neonates: Facial Action and Cry." *Pain* 28 (1987): 395–410.

Gunnar, M., Connors, J., Isensee, J., & Wall, L. "Adrenocortical Activity and Behavioral Distress in Human Newborns." *Developmental Psychobiology* 21 (1988): 297–310.

Gunnar, M., Fisch, R., & Malone, S. "The Effects of a Pacifying Stimulus on Behavioral and Adrenocortical Responses to Circumcision in the Newborn." *Journal of the American Academy of Child Psychiatry* 23: (1984): 34–8.

Gunnar, M., Malone, S., Vance, G., & Fisch, R. "Coping with Aversive Stimulation in the Neonatal Period: Quiet Sleep and Plasma Cortisol Levels during Recovery from Circumcision," *Child Development* 56 (1985): 824–34.

Hall, R. "Epispasm: Circumcision in Reverse." *Moment*, February 1992, 34–7.

Hammond, T. *Awakenings: A Preliminary Poll of Circumcised Males*, 1994. (Available from National Organization to Halt the Abuse and Routine Mutilation of Males, P.O. Box 460795, San Francisco, CA 94146)

Hartman, C. & Burgess, A. "Information Processing of Trauma." *Child Abuse and Neglect* 17 (1993): 47–58.

Hauptman, J. "Images of Women in the Talmud." In R. Ruether, ed., *Religion and Sexism: Images of Women in Jewish and Christian Traditions*. New York: Simon and Schuster, 1974.

Helliker, K. "Anxious Parents Question Merits of Circumcision." *Wall Street Journal*, 28 May 1996, A21.

Hoffman, L. *Covenant of Blood: Circumcision and Gender in Rabbinic Judaism*. Chicago: University of Chicago Press, 1996.

Hosken, F. *The Hosken Report*. Lexington, MA: Women's International Network News, 1993.

Howard, C., Howard, F., & Weitzman, M. "Acetaminophen Analgesis in Neonatal Circumcision: The Effect on Pain." *Pediatrics* 93 (1994): 645.

Kaplan, G. "Complications of Circumcision." *Urological Clinics of North America* 10 (1983): 543–9.

Karsenty, N. "A Mother Questions Brit Milla." *Humanistic Judaism* 16 (1988, summer): 14–21.

Katz. L. "Mitzvah or Mutilation? Circumcision Sparks Debate." *Northern California Jewish Bulletin*, 14 February 1992, 4.

Kaweblum, Y., Press, S., Kogan, L., Levine, M., & Kaweblum, M. "Circumcision Using the Mogen Clamp," *Clinical Pediatrics* 23 (1984): 679–82.

Keating, J. & Brock, T., "Acceptance of Persuasion and the Inhibition of Counterargument under Various Distraction Tasks." *Journal of Experimental Social Psychology* 10 (1974): 301–9.

Kennedy, H. "Trauma in Childhood: Signs and Sequelae as Seen in the Analysis of an Adolescent." *Psychoanalytic Study of the Child* 41 (1986): 209–19.

Klaus, M. & Klaus, P. *The Amazing Newborn*. New York: Addison-Wesley, 1985.

Kosmin, B., Goldstein, S., Waksberg, J., Lerer, N. Keysar, A., & Scheckner, J. *Highlights of the CJF 1990 National Jewish Population Survey*. New York: Council of Jewish Federations, 1991.

Kramer, W. "Denial of Spousal Abuse the Jewish Problem." *Jewish Spectator* (1994, fall): 6–7.

Krohn, P. *Bris Milah*. Brooklyn: Mesorah Publishing, 1985.

Kushner, L. *The River of Light*. San Francisco: Harper & Row, 1981.

*Kushner, M. "Ancient Ritual is Beneficial." *(Philadelphia) Jewish Times*, 21 March 1991.

Laibow, R. "Circumcision and Its Relationship to Attachment Impairment." In *Syllabus of Abstracts*, the Second International Symposium on Circumcision, 1991.(Available from NOCIRC, P.O. Box 2512, San Anselmo, CA 94960)

*Landis, D. & Robbin, S. "Gainful Pain." *Tikkun*, Sept/Oct 1990.

Lewis, J. *In the Name of Humanity*. New York: Eugenics Publishing, 1949.

Loewenstein, R. *Christians and Jews: A Psychoanalytic Study*. New York: International Universities Press, 1951.

Luchins, A., "Focusing on the Object of Judgment in the Social Situation." *Journal of Social Psychology* 60 (1963): 231–49.

Maimonides, M. *Guide for the Perplexed*. New York: Dover Publications (original work published 1190), 1956.

Malone, S., Gunnar, M., & Fisch, R. "Adrenocortical and Behavioral Responses to Limb Restraint in Human Neonates." *Developmental Psychobiology* 18 (1985): 435–46.

Markessinis, J. *The First Week of Life*. Princeton, NJ: Edcom Systems, 1971.

Marshall, R., Stratton, W., Moore, J., & Boxerman, S. "Circumcision: I. Effects upon Newborn Behavior," *Infant Behavior and Development* 3 (1980): 1–14.

Marshall, R., Porter, F., Rogers, A., Moore, J., Anderson, B., & Boxerman, S. "Circumcision: II. Effects upon Mother-Infant Interaction," *Early Human Development* 7 (1982): 367–74.

Maslin, S. *What We Believe, What We Do.* pamphlet. New York: UAHC Press, 1993.

Meyer, M. *Response to Modernity: A History of the Reform Movement in Judaism*. New York: Oxford University Press, 1988.

*Meyer, M. "Berit Milah within the History of the Reform Movement." In L. Barth, ed., *Berit Mila in the Reform Context*. Berit Milah Board of Reform Judaism, 1990.

Meyers, A. "Newborns Feel Pain," letter to the editor. *New York Times*, 29 May 1996, A18.

Milgram, S. "Group Pressure and Action against a Person." *Journal of Abnormal and Social Psychology* 69 (1964): 137–43.

Milos, M. "Infant Circumcision: What I Wish I Had Known." *The Truth Seeker* 1 (July/August 1989): 3.

Milos, M. & Macris, D. "Circumcision: A Medical or a Human Rights Issue?" *Journal of Nurse-Midwifery* 37 (Supplement, 1992): 87S-96S.

Money, J. & Davison, J. "Adult Penile Circumcision: Erotosexual and Cosmetic Sequelae." *Journal of Sex Research* 19 (1983): 289-92.

Montagu, A. *Sex, Man, and Society*. New York: G. P. Putnam's Sons, 1969.

Morgan, W. "The Rape of the Phallus." *Journal of the American Medical Association* 193 (1965): 223–4.

Morgenstern, J. *Rites of Birth, Marriage, Death and Kindred Occasions*. Cincinnati: Hebrew Union College Press, 1966.

Moss, L. "Circumcision: A Jewish Inquiry." *Midstream*, January 1992, 20–3.

National Center for Health Statistics. 6525 Belcrest Rd., Hyattsville, MD 20782 (301)436-8500.

Newman, R. "Circumcision: The False Initiation." *Changing Men*, Fall/Winter 1991, 19–21.

NOCIRC Newsletter. Fall 1990, 3.

O'Mara, P., ed., *Circumcision: The Rest of the Story*. Santa Fe, NM: Mothering, 1993.

Ostwald, P. & Peltzman, P. "The Cry of the Human Infant." *Scientific American* 230 (1974): 85.

Owens, M., & Todt, E. "Pain in Infancy: Neonatal Reaction to a Heel Lance." *Pain* 20 (1984): 77–86.

Paige, K. "The Ritual of Circumcision." *Human Nature*, May 1978, 42.

Parsons, M. "The Beginning," *Ashbury (NJ) Park Press*, 3 February 1996, B1.

Philipson, D. *The Reform Movement in Judaism*. 1931. Reprint. New York: Ktav Publishers, 1967.

Pickard-Ginsburg. M. "Jesse's Circumcision," letter to the editor. *Mothering*, Spring 1979, 80.

Pollack, M. "Circumcision: A Jewish Feminist Perspective." In K. Weiner & A. Moon, eds., *Jewish Women Speak Out*. Seattle, WA: Canopy Press, 1995.

Porter, F., Miller, R., & Marshall, R. "Neonatal Pain Cries: Effect of Circumcision on Acoustic Features and Perceived Urgency." *Child Development* 57 (1986): 790–802.

Pugh, L. "Santa Fe Nurses Rejects Circumcisions." *Albuquerque Journal*, 13 June 1995, 1.

Rabinowitz, R. & Hulbert, W. "Newborn Circumcision Should Not Be Performed without Anesthesia." *Birth* 22 (1995): 45–6.

Raisbeck, B. "Circumcision: A Wound Which Lasts a Lifetime." *Healing Currents*, 1993, 21.

*Raul-Friedman, E. "A Rebuttal—Circumcision: A Jewish Legacy." *Midstream*, May 1992, 31.

Richards, M., Bernal, J., & Brackbill, Y. "Early Behavioral Differences: Gender or Circumcision?" *Developmental Psychobiology* 9 (1976): 89-95.

Ritter, T. *Say No to Circumcision*. Aptos, CA: Hourglass, 1992.

Roberts, M. "Shear Bris." *Denver Westword*, 24 February 1993, 23.

Romain, J. "Keeping the Faith." *Jewish Chronicle,* 23 Feb. 1996, 28.

*Romberg, H. *Bris Milah*. New York: Feldheim, 1982.

Romberg, R. *Circumcision: The Painful Dilemma*. South Hadley, MA: Bergin & Garvey, 1985.

Romberg, R. "Circumcision Feedback," letter to the editor. *Mensa Bulletin*, May 1993.

*Romirowsky, S. "Psycho-Social Aspects of Brit Milah." *Conservative Judaism*, Summer 1990, 41-5.

*Roth, J. "The Meaning for Today." *Moment*, February 1992, 41-4.

Ruby, W. "Reform vs. Conservative: Who's Winning?" Moment, April 1996, 32.

Ryan, C. & Finer, N. "Changing Attitudes and Practices Regarding Local Analgesia for Newborn Circumcision." *Pediatrics* 94 (1994): 230-3.

Schacter-Shalomi, Z. *The First Step*. New York: Bantam, 1983.

Schäfer, P. *Judeophobia: Attitudes toward the Jews in the Ancient World.* Cambridge, MA: Harvard University Press, 1997.

Schechter, N. "The Undertreatment of Pain in Children: An Overview." *Pediatric Clinics of North America* 36 (1989): 781–94.

Schonfeld, V. "First Cut is the Unkindest." *The Guardian*, 20 September 1995, 5.

Schonfeld, V. "It's a Boy," documentary on circumcision. Ch. 4, England, 21 September 1995.

Schonfeld, V. & Bard, J. "Severing the Chain." *The Jewish Quarterly*, winter 1995, 27–31.

Schultz, T., "A Nurse's View on Circumcision." In P. O'Mara, ed., *Circumcision: The Rest of the Story.* Santa Fe, NM: Mothering, 1993, 80-1.

Scott, L. "The Unkindest Cut? Opponents of Circumcision Question Necessity of Jewish Rite." *The Jewish Community Voice*, 30 August 1995, 9–10.

Sexty, L. "Jared's Ordeal." In P. O'Mara, ed., *Circumcision: The Rest of the Story.* Santa Fe, NM: Mothering, 1994.

"Shattering the Myth: Developing an Orthodox Response to Domestic Violence," *The Jewish Advocate*, 20-26 Dec. 1996, 33.

Sherif, M. "Conformity-Deviation, Norms, and Group Relations." In I. Berg & B. Bass, eds., *Conformity and Deviation.* New York: Harper, 1961, 59–181.

Sherman, M. & Sherman, I. "Sensori-Motor Responses in Infants." *Journal of Comparative Psychology* 5 (1925): 53–68.

Silverman, J. "Circumcision: The Delicate Dilemma." *The Jewish Monthly*, November 1991, 31.

*Singer, S. "The Pain and the Pleasure." *Moment*, February 1992, 38–40.

*Spock, B. *The Common Sense Book of Baby and Child Care.* New York: Duell, Sloan, and Pearce, 1946.

Spock, B. & Rothenberg, M. *Dr. Spock's Baby and Child Care.* New York: Pocket Books, 1992.

Stang, H., Gunnar, M., Snellman, L., Condon, L., & Kestenbaum, R. "Local Anesthesia for Neonatal Circumcision." *Journal of the American Medical Association* 259 (1988): 1507–11.

*Steinberg, J. "Government Wants Community to Justify Ritual Circumcision." *Australian Jewish News, Queensland Edition*, 28 January 1994, 1.

Steinberg, M. *Basic Judaism* (rev. ed.). New York: Harcourt Brace Jovanovich, 1975.

Stewart, D. *Theordor Herzl.* Garden City, NY: Doubleday, 1974.

Susskind, J. "Circumcision is Cruel and Harmful," letter to the editor. *Moment.* June 1992.

Taddio, A., Goldbach, M., Ipp, M., Stevens, B., & Koren, G. "Effect of Neonatal Circumcision on Pain Responses during Vaccination of Boys." *The Lancet* 345 (1995): 291–2.

Taddio, A., Katz, J., Ilersich, A., & Koren, G. "Effect of Neonatal Circumcision on Pain Response during Subsequent Routine Vaccination." *The Lancet* 349 (1997): 599–603

Taylor, J., Lockwood, A., & Taylor, A. "The Prepuce: Specialized Mucosa of the Penis and Its Loss to Circumcision." *British Journal of Urology* 77 (1996): 291–5.

Terr, L. "What Happens to Early Memories of Trauma?" *Journal of the American Academy of Child and Adolescent Psychiatry* 27 (1988): 96–104.

Terr, L. "Childhood Traumas: An Outline and Overview." *American Journal of Psychiatry* 148 (1991): 10-20.

"The Unkindest Cut of All," letter to the editor, *Playgirl*, July 1979, 108.

Union of American Hebrew Congregations. Programs and Services brochure. New York, August 1990.

van der Kolk, B. *Psychological Trauma*. Washington, DC: American Psychiatric Press, 1987.

van der Kolk, B. "The Compulsion to Repeat the Trauma: Re-Enactment, Revictimization, and Masochism." *Psychiatric Clinics of North America 12* (1989): 389–411.

Walco, G., Cassidy, R., & Schechter, N. "Pain, Hurt, and Harm: The Ethics of Pain Control in Infants and Children." *New England Journal of Medicine* 331 (1994): 541–4.

Walker, B. *The Crone: Woman of Age, Wisdom, and Power*. San Francisco: Harper Collins, 1985.

Wallerstein, E. *Circumcision: An American Health Fallacy*. New York: Springer Publishing, 1980.

Wallerstein, E. "Circumcision: The Uniquely American Medical Enigma." *Symposium on Advances in Pediatric Urology, Urologic Clinics of North America* 12 (1985): 123-32.

Warren, J. et al. "Circumcision of Children," *British Medical Journal* 312 (1996): 377.

Weill, T. "Anti-Semitism: Selected Psychodynamic Insights." *American Journal of Psychoanalysis* 41 (1981): 139–48..

Weiss, R. Quoted in S. Church, "Jewish Rite of Brit Milah: Giving Thanks for a Birth." *Binghamton (NY) Press & SunBulletin*, 27 April 1986.

Williamson, P. & Williamson, M. "Physiologic Stress Reduction by a Local Anesthetic during Newborn Circumcision," *Pediatrics* 71 (1983): 40.

Wilson, J. *Trauma, Transformation, and Healing*. New York: Brunner/Mazel, 1989.

Wine, S. "Circumcision." *Humanistic Judaism* 16 (1988, summer): 4–8.

Wiswell, T., Smith, F., & Bass, J. "Decreased Incidence of Urinary Tract Infections in Circumcised Male Infants." *Pediatrics* 75 (1985): 901–3.

Wiswell, T., Enzenauer, R., Holton, M., Cornish, J., & Hanskins, C. "Declining Frequency of Circumcision: Implications for Changes in the Absolute Incidence and Male to Female Sex Ratio of Urinary Tract Infection in Early Infancy." *Pediatrics* 79 (1987): 338–42.

Zeskind, P., & Marshall, T. "The Relation between Variations in Pitch and Maternal Perceptions of Infant Crying." *Child Development* 59 (1988): 193–6.

Index

Addendum

There is a new public campaign in Israel to ban circumcision. The effort is lead by a nonprofit organization whose charter calls for bringing an end "to the primitive act of circumcision." One of the leaders called circumcision "a violent act against the infants." The group distributes literature urging Israelis not to circumcise their sons.*

---

* This text is based on a May 5, 1997, news item that appeared on the SNS News Service (Israel).

ORDER FORM

[   ] CIRCUMCISION: THE HIDDEN TRAUMA $18.95
     Ronald Goldman, Ph.D.   Foreword by Ashley Montagu, Ph.D.

A revealing, intensive exploration of the unrecognized psychological and social aspects of circumcision. *Circumcision: The Hidden Trauma* has been endorsed by professionals in the fields of psychology, psychiatry, child development, pediatrics, obstetrics, childbirth education, sociology, and anthropology.

> This provocative analysis of circumcision's potential impact on men and gender relations merits serious attention.   —Patricia Yancey Martin, Ph.D.,
> Professor of Sociology, Florida State University

[   ] QUESTIONING CIRCUMCISION: $11.95
     A JEWISH PERSPECTIVE
     Ronald Goldman, Ph.D.

Call toll-free 1-888-445-5199 for credit card orders.
For mail orders, please print clearly.

Send me copies of the above titles. (Indicate quantities in brackets.)

Name _____

Address _____

City _____ State _____ Zip _____

Daytime Phone _____

Shipping and handling is $3.00 for first copy, $1.00 for each additional copy. Massachusetts residents add 5% sales tax.

Total enclosed $ _____ (U.S. dollars only)

Make checks payable to and send to:

     Vanguard Publications
     P.O. Box 8055
     Boston, MA 02114   (Bulk discounts available.)

If you want us to send information to a friend or colleague, please include his or her name and address.

Prices subject to change without notice. Allow 2–4 weeks for delivery.